The Rule of St Benedict

Translated by
Justin McCann

Sheed and Ward
London

Copyright © 1970, 1976 by Sheed & Ward Ltd. First published 1952 by Burns & Oates Ltd. This edition first published 1976, third impression 1980. ISBN 0 7220 7621 5. All rights reserved. *Nihil obstat* J. Arendzen, Censor. *Imprimatur* E. Morrogh Bernard, Vicar General, Westminster, 26 February 1951. Printed in Great Britain for Sheed and Ward Ltd, 6 Blenheim Street, London W1Y 0SA by Biddles Ltd, Guildford, Surrey.

THE RULE OF
ST BENEDICT

οὐ γὰρ περὶ τοῦ ἐπιτυχόντος ὁ λόγος,
ἀλλὰ περὶ τοῦ ὅντινα τρόπον χρὴ ζῆν.

PLATO, *Republic* 352 D.

PREFACE

SAINT BENEDICT lived and worked in central Italy in the first half of the sixth century, the approximate date of his death being A.D. 547. His life began and ended with periods of devastating war, during which Italy was gravely disorganized; but at its centre, under the masterful rule of Theodoric (493-526), it knew some thirty years of peace. Yet this period too, though free from the alarms and excursions of war, was not one in which the arts of peace flourished greatly, so that we cannot be surprised that the slender chronicles of the time contain no record of the Saint's life and work. It is not until nearly fifty years after his death that we have any record of him, i.e. until the year 594 and the *Dialogues* of Pope St Gregory the Great. However, this record, when it came, was certainly an appreciative one, and it contains an item which is of particular interest and value to an editor of the Holy Rule. Here is the important piece of information that St Gregory gives his deacon:

I should like, Peter, to tell you much more about this venerable abbot; but I purposely pass over some of his deeds, for I hasten to get on to the lives of others. Yet I would not have you ignorant of this, that Benedict was eminent, not only for the many miracles that made him famous, but also for his teaching. In fact, he wrote a Rule for Monks, which is of conspicuous discretion and is written in a lucid style. If anyone wishes to know Benedict's character and life more precisely, he may find a complete account of his principles and practice in the ordinances of that Rule; for the Saint cannot have taught otherwise than as he lived (II 36).

Such is the testimony of the greatest of all the disciples of the Rule, who introduced it into that monastery of his whence came the apostles of the English people, who commended it regularly in his letters, and whose advocacy it was that set the Rule upon the career which resulted in its becoming the monastic code of Western Europe.

When did St Benedict compose his Rule? He would have felt the need of some code of law from the very beginning, as soon as he had accepted the task of organizing community life, that is to say, at Subiaco and in the earliest years of the sixth century. It is necessary to suppose, for instance, that his first communities had a definite horarium for the Divine Office, for study, and for manual work, that they had officials and a discipline of punishments for breaches of monastic rule, etc. It is probable, therefore, that the corresponding chapters of the Rule were established, at least in substance, as early as this. In fact, it seems very reasonable to suppose that St Benedict composed his Rule, so to say, "as he went along", adding from year to year the conclusions suggested by experience and by his monastic reading, and in this gradual way constructing finally a complete code of monastic observance. The Rule itself contains various indications which support such a theory of progressive composition. Although there is, of course, a fundamental continuity of subject-matter, yet there are not a few chapters which occur in a somewhat haphazard fashion and according to no easily recognizable plan. In contrast with these are several compact groups of chapters, held together in so close and self-contained a manner by their unity of subject, as to suggest strongly that they had previously enjoyed an independent existence. The chief groups of this sort are the eight chapters on faults and their punishment (the *Strafkodex*, as the Germans call it) and the eleven chapters which determine the substance and ritual of the Divine Office. This latter group of chapters is noteworthy for the abundance of its "vulgarisms", i.e. the forms and usages of popular Latin, a circumstance which would persuade us—a thing otherwise likely—that it is the most primitive portion of the Rule. Opposed to these compact groups are the numerous chapters which occur in an accidental fashion and have in some cases the air of postscripts or supplements. There is a postscript of this sort in connexion with the important matter of the abbot and his necessary qualities. The topic is dealt with professedly in the second chapter, but is resumed and supplemented, towards the end of the Rule, in the sixty-fourth. There is a specially interesting indication in the sixty-sixth chapter, which ends with a sentence that is plainly a terminal one, marking the final point of one draft of the Rule. Then there came a second draft, with seven additional chapters. And so the work was completed. We may guess that this consummation was reached towards the end of the Saint's life, perhaps in the decade 530-40. And then the Rule left St Benedict's hands to be launched sooner or later upon the world of western monachism. It was welcomed, for western monachism needed just such a Rule. It may perhaps be construed as a proof of the sincerity of the welcome that it took the form, at a very early date, of a comprehensive revision of the Rule's latinity.

The English translation was made by me at Oxford, at the request of the Lady Abbess of Stanbrook. The first edition, printed and published at Stanbrook in 1937, is now out of print, and I have kindly been allowed, for the purposes of the present book, to issue the translation in this, its second edition. It has been carefully revised throughout, and I trust that I have succeeded in making it an accurate and readable version of the Rule. Some readers may be puzzled by the dates which accompany the Rule, section by section. They are for the guidance of the Lector at the monastic Office of Prime, and they provide for a threefold annual recitation of the Rule. The custom is a very ancient one, deriving from St Benedict's regulation (c.58) that his novices should have the Rule read to them three times during their year's noviciate: *Ecce lex sub qua militare vis.* . . To hear the Rule read thus, day by day and over a long stretch of years, naturally makes it a familiar text, very intimately known. It also encourages the conviction that the Rule needs little commendation and is best left to speak for itself. So I now stand aside and give it free passage, save only for Plato's sentence:

It is no chance topic that engages us, for our subject is: How shall a man order his life?

CONTENTS OF THE RULE

CONTENTS

CONTENTS

CONTENTS

THE TEXT OF THE RULE

SAINT BENEDICT'S
RULE FOR MONKS

PROLOGUE

EARKEN, my son, to the precepts of the master and
incline the ear of thy heart; freely accept and
faithfully fulfil the instructions of a loving father,
that by the labour of obedience thou mayest return to him
from whom thou hast strayed by the sloth of disobedience.
To thee are my words now addressed, whosoever thou
mayest be that renouncing thine own will to fight for the true
King, Christ, dost take up the strong and glorious weapons
of obedience.

nd first of all, whatever good work thou undertakest,
ask him with most instant prayer to perfect it, so that he who
has deigned to count us among his sons may never be pro-
voked by our evil conduct. For we must always so serve him
with the gifts which he has given us, that he may never as an
angry father disinherit his children, nor yet as a dread lord
be driven by our sins to cast into everlasting punishment the
wicked servants who would not follow him to glory.

p with us then at last, for the Scripture arouseth us,
saying: *Now is the hour for us to rise from sleep.*[1] Let us open our
eyes to the divine light, and let us hear with attentive ears
the warning that the divine voice crieth daily to us: *Today if
ye will hear his voice, harden not your hearts.*[2] And again: *He
that hath ears to hear, let him hear what the Spirit saith to the
churches.*[3] And what doth he say? *Come, ye children, hearken*

Jan. 1
May 2
Sept. 1

Jan. 2
May 3
Sept. 2

[1] Rom. xiii. 11. [2] Ps. xciv. 8. [3] Mat. xi. 15; Apoc. ii. 7.

1

unto me: I will teach you the fear of the Lord.[1] *Run while ye have the light of life, lest the darkness of death overtake you.*[2]

Jan. 3
May 4
Sept. 3

And the Lord, seeking his workman among the multitudes to whom he thus crieth, saith again: *What man is he that desireth life and would fain see good days?*[3] And if hearing him thou answer, "I am he," God saith to thee: *If thou wilt have true and everlasting life, keep thy tongue from evil and thy lips that they speak no guile. Turn away from evil and do good: seek after peace and pursue it.*[4] And when you have done these things, my eyes will be upon you and my ears open unto your prayers. And before you call upon me, I shall say to you, "Lo, here I am." What can be sweeter to us, dearest brethren, than this voice of our Lord inviting us? Behold in his loving mercy the Lord showeth us the way of life.

Jan. 4
May 5
Sept. 4

Let us, therefore, gird our loins with faith and the performance of good works, and following the guidance of the Gospel walk in his paths, so that we may merit to see him who has called us unto his kingdom. And, if we wish to dwell in the tabernacle of his kingdom, except we run thither with good deeds we shall not arrive. But let us ask the Lord with the prophet: *Lord, who shall dwell in thy tabernacle, or who shall rest upon thy holy hill?*[5] Then, brethren, let us hear the Lord answering and showing us the way to that tabernacle and saying: *He that walketh without blemish and doth that which is right; he that speaketh truth in his heart, who hath used no deceit in his tongue, nor done evil to his neighbour, nor believed ill of his neighbour.*[6] He that taketh the evil spirit that tempteth him, and casteth him and his temptation from

---

[1] Ps. xxxiii. 12. [2] John xii. 35. [3] Ps. xxxiii. 13. [4] Ibid. 14-16.
[5] Ps. xiv. 1. [6] Ibid. 2, 3.

the sight of his heart, and bringeth him to naught; who graspeth his evil suggestions as they arise and dasheth them to pieces on the rock that is Christ.[1] Such men as these, fearing the Lord, are not puffed up on account of their good works, but judging that they can do no good of themselves and that all cometh from God, they magnify the Lord's work in them, using the word of the prophet: *Not unto us, O Lord, not unto us, but unto thy name give the glory.*[2] So the apostle Paul imputed nothing of his preaching to himself, but said: *By the grace of God I am what I am.*[3] And again he saith: *He that glorieth, let him glory in the Lord.*[4]

Wherefore the Lord also saith in the Gospel: *He that heareth these my words and doth them, shall be likened to a wise man that built his house upon a rock. The floods came and the winds blew, and they beat upon that house, and it fell not, for it was founded upon a rock.*[5] Having given us these instructions, the Lord daily expects us to make our life correspond with his holy admonitions. And the days of our life are lengthened and a respite allowed us for this very reason, that we may amend our evil ways. For the Apostle saith: *Knowest thou not that the patience of God inviteth thee to repentance?*[6] For the merciful Lord saith: *I will not the death of a sinner, but that he should be converted and live.*[7]

Jan. 5
May 6
Sept. 5

So, brethren, we have asked the Lord about the dwellers in his tabernacle and have heard what is the duty of him who would dwell therein; it remains for us to fulfil this duty. Therefore our hearts and bodies must be made ready to fight under the holy obedience of his commands; and let us ask

Jan. 6
May 7
♣Sept. 6

[1] *Cf.* Ps. cxxxvi. 9. [2] Ps. cxiii. 9. [3] 1 Cor. xv. 10. [4] 2 Cor. x. 17.
[5] Mat. vii. 24, 25. [6] Rom. ii. 4. [7] Ezech. xxxiii. 11.

God that he be pleased, where our nature is powerless, to give us the help of his grace. And if we would escape the pains of hell and reach eternal life, then must we—while there is still time, while we are in this body and can fulfil all these things by the light of this life—hasten to do now what may profit us for eternity.

Jan. 7
May 8
Sept. 7

Therefore must we establish a school of the Lord's service; in founding which we hope to ordain nothing that is harsh or burdensome. But if, for good reason, for the amendment of evil habit or the preservation of charity, there be some strictness of discipline, do not be at once dismayed and run away from the way of salvation, of which the entrance must needs be narrow. But, as we progress in our monastic life and in faith, our hearts shall be enlarged, and we shall run with unspeakable sweetness of love in the way of God's commandments; so that, never abandoning his rule but persevering in his teaching in the monastery until death, we shall share by patience in the sufferings of Christ, that we may deserve to be partakers also of his kingdom. Amen.

END OF THE PROLOGUE

I

THE KINDS
OF MONKS

THERE are evidently four kinds of monks. The first are
the Cenobites, that is those who live in monasteries,
serving under a rule and an abbot.

Jan. 8
May 9
Sept. 8

The second are the Anchorites or Hermits, that is those
who not in the first fervour of their conversion, but after
long probation in a monastery, having learnt in association
with many brethren how to fight against the devil, go out
well-armed from the ranks of the community to the solitary
combat of the desert. They are able now to live without the
help of others, and by their own strength and God's assistance to fight against the temptations of mind and body.

The third kind of monks is that detestable one of the
Sarabaites, who not having been tested, as gold in the fur-
nace, by any rule or by the lessons of experience, are as soft
and yielding as lead. In their actions they still conform to the
standards of the world, so that their tonsure marks them as
liars before God. They live in twos or threes, or even singly,
without a shepherd, in their own sheepfolds and not in the
Lord's. Their law is their own good pleasure: whatever
they think of or choose to do, that they call holy; what they
like not, that they regard as unlawful.

Jan. 9
May 10
Sept. 9

The fourth kind of monks are those called Gyrovagues.
These spend their whole lives wandering from province to
province, staying three days in one monastery and four in
another, ever roaming and never stable, given up to their

own wills and the allurements of gluttony, and worse in all respects than the Sarabaites.

Of the wretched observance of all these folk it is better to be silent than to speak. Therefore, leaving them on one side, let us proceed with God's help to provide for the strong race of the Cenobites.

CHAPTER

2

WHAT KIND OF
MAN THE ABBOT
SHOULD BE

Jan. 10
May 11
Sept.10

A N abbot who is worthy to rule a monastery should always remember what he is called and realize in his actions the name of a superior. For he is believed to be the representative of Christ in the monastery, and for that reason is called by a name of his, according to the words of the Apostle : *Ye have received the spirit of the adoption of sons, whereby we cry Abba, Father.*[1] Therefore the abbot ought not to teach, or ordain, or command anything which is against the law of the Lord; on the contrary, his commands and teaching should be infused into the minds of his disciples like the leaven of divine justice. Let the abbot remember always that at the dread Judgement of God there will be an examination of both these matters, of his teaching and of the obedience of his disciples. And let the abbot realize that the shepherd will have to answer for any lack of profit which the Father of the family may discover in his sheep. On the other hand, if the shepherd have spent all diligence on an unruly and disobedient flock and devoted his utmost care to.

[1] Rom. viii. 15.

the amending of its vicious ways, then he will be acquitted at the Judgement and may say to the Lord with the prophet: *I have not hid thy justice within my heart: I have declared thy truth and thy salvation;*[1] *but they have despised and rejected me.*[2] And so at the last, for these sheep disobedient to his care, let death itself bring its penalty.

Therefore, when anyone has received the name of abbot, he ought to rule his disciples with a twofold teaching, displaying all goodness and holiness by deeds and by words, but by deeds rather than by words. To intelligent disciples let him expound the Lord's commandments in words; but to those of harder hearts and ruder minds let him show forth the divine precepts by his example. And whatever he has taught his disciples to be contrary to God's law, let him show by his example that it is not to be done, lest while preaching to others he should himself become a castaway, and lest God should some day say to him in his sin: *Why dost thou repeat my commandments by rote, and boast of my covenant with thee? For thou hast hated to amend thy life and hast cast my words behind thee.*[3] And again: *Thou sawest the speck of dust in thy brother's eye and didst not see the beam in thy own.*[4]

Jan. 11
May 12
Sept. 11

Let him not make any distinction of persons in the monastery. Let him not love one more than another, unless he find him better in good works and obedience. Let not a freeborn monk be put before one that was a slave, unless there be some other reasonable ground for it. But if the abbot, for just reason, think fit so to do, let him fix anyone's order as he will; otherwise let them keep their due places; because, whether slaves or freemen, we are all one in Christ, and have to serve alike in the army of the same Lord. *For there is*

Jan. 12
May 13
Sept. 12

[1] Ps. xxxix. 11.   [2] Is. i. 2.   [3] Ps. xlix. 16, 17.   [4] *Cf.* Mat. vii. 3.

7

no respect of persons with God.[1] In this regard only are we dis-
tinguished in his sight, if we be found better than others in
good works and humility. Therefore let the abbot show an
equal love to all, and let the same discipline be imposed on
all in accordance with their deserts.

Jan. 13
May 14
Sept. 13
For the abbot in his teaching ought always to observe the
rule of the apostle, wherein he says: *Reprove, persuade, rebuke.*[2] He must adapt himself to circumstances, now using
severity and now persuasion, displaying the rigour of a
master or the loving kindness of a father. That is to say, that
he must sternly rebuke the undisciplined and restless; but
the obedient, meek, and patient, these he should exhort to
advance in virtue. As for the negligent and rebellious, we
warn him to reprimand and punish them. And let him not
shut his eyes to the faults of offenders; but as soon as they
begin to appear, let him, as he can, cut them out by the
roots, mindful of the fate of Heli, the priest of Silo. Those
of gentle disposition and good understanding should be
punished, for the first and second time, by verbal admonition; but bold, hard, proud, and disobedient characters
should be checked at the very beginning of their ill-doing
by the rod and corporal punishment, according to the text:
The fool is not corrected with words;[3] and again: *Beat thy son with
the rod and thou shalt deliver his soul from death.*[4]

Jan. 14
May 15
Sept. 14
The abbot should always remember what he is and what
he is called, and should know that to whom more is committed, from him more is required. Let him realize also how
difficult and arduous a task he has undertaken, of ruling souls
and adapting himself to many dispositions. One he must

[1] Rom. ii. 11.   [2] 2 Tim. iv. 2.   [3] Prov. xviii. 2; xxix. 19.
[4] Ibid. xxiii. 14.

8

humour, another rebuke, another persuade, according to each one's disposition and understanding, and thus adapt and accommodate himself to all in such a way, that he may not only suffer no loss in the sheep committed to him, but may even rejoice in the increase of a good flock.

Above all let him not have greater solicitude for fleeting, earthly, and perishable things, and so overlook or undervalue the salvation of the souls committed to him; but let him always remember that he has undertaken the government of souls and will have to give an account of them. And if he be tempted to complain of lack of means, let him remember the words: *Seek ye first the kingdom of God and his approval, and all these things shall be yours without the asking.*[1] And again: *Those that fear him never go wanting.*[2] And let him know that he who has undertaken the government of souls, must prepare himself to render an account of them. And whatever number of brethren he knows he has under his care, let him regard it as certain that he will have to give the Lord an account of all these souls on the Day of Judgement, and certainly of his own soul also. And thus, fearing always the examination which the shepherd will have to face for the sheep entrusted to him, and anxious regarding the account which will have to be given for others, he is made solicitous for his own sake also; and while by his admonitions helping others to amend, he himself is cleansed of his faults.

Jan. 15
May 16
Sept. 15

[1] Mat. vi. 33.   [2] Ps. xxxiii. 10.

CHAPTER

3

OF CALLING
THE BRETHREN
TO COUNCIL

Jan. 16
May 17
Sept. 16

As often as any important business has to be done in the monastery, let the abbot call together the whole community and himself set forth the matter. And, having heard the advice of the brethren, let him take counsel with himself and then do what he shall judge to be most expedient. Now the reason why we have said that all should be called to council, is that God often reveals what is better to the younger. Let the brethren give their advice with all deference and humility, nor venture to defend their opinions obstinately; but let the decision depend rather on the abbot's judgement, so that when he has decided what is the better course, all may obey. However, just as it is proper for disciples to obey their master, so is it becoming that he on his part should dispose all things with prudence and justice.

Jan. 17
May 18
Sept. 17

In all things, therefore, let all follow the Rule as master, nor let anyone rashly depart from it. Let no one in the monastery follow the will of his own heart; nor let anyone presume to contend impudently with his abbot, or to contend with him at all when outside the monastery. Should he presume to do so, let him undergo the discipline of the Rule. The abbot himself, however, should do all things in the fear of God and observance of the Rule, knowing that he will certainly have to render an account of all his judgements to God, the most just Judge. But if the business to be done in the interests of the monastery be of lesser importance, let him use the advice of the seniors only. It is written: *Do all things with counsel, and thy deeds shall not bring thee repentance.*[1]

[1] Ecclus. xxxii. 24.

CHAPTER
4

THE TOOLS OF
GOOD WORKS

IN the first place, to love the Lord God with all one's
heart, all one's soul, and all one's strength.
Then, one's neighbour as oneself.

Jan. 18
May 19
Sept.18

Then not to kill.

Not to commit adultery.

Not to steal.

Not to covet.

Not to bear false witness.

To honour all men.

Not to do to another what one would not have done to oneself.

To deny oneself, in order to follow Christ.

To chastise the body.

Not to seek soft living.

To love fasting.

To relieve the poor.

To clothe the naked.

To visit the sick.

To bury the dead.

To help the afflicted.

To console the sorrowing.

To avoid worldly conduct.

To prefer nothing to the love of Christ.

Not to yield to anger.

Not to nurse a grudge.

Not to hold guile in one's heart.

Not to make a feigned peace.

Jan. 19
May 20
Sept.19

11

Not to forsake charity.

Not to swear, lest perchance one forswear oneself.

To utter truth from heart and mouth.

Not to render evil for evil.

To do no wrong to anyone, and to bear patiently wrongs done to oneself.

To love one's enemies.

Not to render cursing for cursing, but rather blessing.

To bear persecution for justice' sake.

Not to be proud.

Not a wine-bibber.

Not a glutton.

Not somnolent.

Not slothful.

Not a grumbler.

Not a detractor.

To put one's hope in God.

To attribute to God, and not to self, whatever good one sees in oneself.

But to recognize always that the evil is one's own doing, and to impute it to oneself.

Jan. 20 To fear the Day of Judgement.

May 21 To dread hell.

Sept. 20 To desire eternal life with all spiritual longing.

To keep death daily before one's eyes.

To keep constant guard over the actions of one's life.

To know for certain that God sees one everywhere.

When evil thoughts come into one's heart, to dash them at once on the rock of Christ and to manifest them to one's spiritual father.

To keep one's mouth from evil and depraved talk.

Not to love much speaking.

Not to speak vain words or such as move to laughter.

Not to love much or violent laughter.

To listen gladly to holy reading.

To apply oneself frequently to prayer.

Daily in one's prayer, with tears and sighs, to confess one's past sins to God.

To amend those sins for the future.

Not to fulfil the desires of the flesh.

To hate one's own will.

To obey in all things the commands of the abbot, even though he himself (which God forbid) should act otherwise: remembering the Lord's precept: *What they say, do ye; but what they do, do ye not.*[1]

Not to wish to be called holy before one is holy; but first to be holy, that one may more truly be called so.

To fulfil God's commandments daily in one's deeds.   Jan. 21

To love chastity.   May 22

To hate no man.   Sept. 21

Not to be jealous.

Not to give way to envy.

Not to love contention.

To shun vainglory.

To reverence the old.

To love the young.

To pray for one's enemies in the love of Christ.

To make peace with one's adversary before sundown.

And never to despair of God's mercy.

Behold these are the tools of the spiritual craft. If we employ them unceasingly day and night, and on the Day of Judgement render account of them, then we shall receive

[1] Mat. xxiii. 3.

13

from the Lord in return that reward which he himself has promised: *Eye hath not seen nor ear heard, what God hath prepared for those that love him.*[1] Now the workshop, wherein we shall diligently execute all these tasks, is the enclosure of the monastery and stability in the community.

CHAPTER

5

OF OBEDIENCE

THE first degree of humility is obedience without delay. This becometh those who hold nothing dearer to them than Christ. Because of the holy service which they have professed, the fear of hell, and the glory of life everlasting, as soon as anything has been ordered by the superior, they receive it as a divine command and cannot suffer any delay in executing it. Of these doth the Lord say: *He hath listened to me and hath obeyed me.*[2] And again he saith to teachers: *He who listens to you, listens to me.*[3]

Such as these, therefore, immediately abandoning their own affairs and forsaking their own will, dropping the work they were engaged on and leaving it unfinished, with swift obedience follow up with their deeds the voice of him who commands them. And almost in the same moment of time that the master's order is issued, is the disciple's work completed, in the swiftness of the fear of the Lord; the two things being rapidly accomplished together by those who are impelled by the desire of attaining life everlasting. Therefore they choose the narrow way, according to the Lord's words: *Narrow is the way which leadeth unto life*;[4] so that not living by their own will, and obeying their own

[1] 1 Cor. ii. 9.   [2] Ps. xvii. 45.   [3] Luke x. 16.   [4] Mat. vii. 14.

desires and passions, but walking by another's judgement and orders, they dwell in monasteries, and desire to have an abbot over them. Assuredly such as these imitate that saying of the Lord wherein he saith: *I came not to do my own will, but the will of him who sent me.*[1]

But this obedience itself will then be acceptable to God and pleasing to men, if what is commanded be not done timorously, or tardily, or tepidly, nor with murmuring or the raising of objections. For the obedience which is given to superiors is given to God, since he himself said: *He who listens to you, listens to me.*[2] And disciples should give their obedience with a good will, because *God loveth a cheerful giver.*[3] For if the disciple obey with an ill will, and murmur not only in words but even in his heart, then even though he fulfil the command, his work will not be acceptable to God, who sees that his heart is murmuring. For work such as this he will gain no reward; nay, rather, he will incur the punishment due to murmurers, unless he amend and make reparation.

Jan. 23
May 24
Sept. 23

CHAPTER

6

OF SILENCE

LET us do as saith the prophet: *I said, I will take heed unto my ways, that I offend not with my tongue. I have set a guard to my mouth. I was dumb and was humbled, and kept silence even from good words.*[4] Here the prophet teaches us that if we should at times, for the love of silence, refrain from good talk, we should with more reason still, for fear of sin's

Jan. 24
May 25
Sept. 24

[1] John vi. 38.   [2] Luke x. 16.   [3] 2 Cor. ix. 7.   [4] Ps. xxxviii. 2, 3.

punishment, eschew all evil talk. Therefore, on account of the great value of silence, let leave to speak be seldom granted to observant disciples, even though it be for good, holy, and edifying conversations; for it is written: *In much speaking thou shalt not escape sin,*[1] and elsewhere: *Death and life are in the power of the tongue.*[2] For it becometh the master to speak and to teach; but it befits the disciple to be silent and to listen.

And therefore, if there be anything to be asked from the superior, let it be sought with all humility and respectful submission. But as for buffoonery and talk that is vain and stirs laughter, we condemn such things everywhere with a perpetual ban, and forbid the disciple to open his mouth for such conversation.

CHAPTER

7

OF HUMILITY

Jan. 25
May 26
Sept. 25

Holy Scripture crieth out to us, brethren, saying: *Everyone that exalteth himself shall be humbled, and he that humbleth himself shall be exalted.*[3] When it so speaks, it teaches us that all exaltation is a kind of pride; which the prophet shows that he shunned in the words: *Lord, my heart is not exalted nor mine eyes lifted up; neither have I dwelt on high things, nor on marvels that are beyond my reach. And why? If I was not humbly minded but exalted my soul with pride; as a child that is weaned from his mother, so wilt thou requite my soul.*[4]

---

[1] Prov. x. 19.   [2] Ibid. xviii. 21.   [3] Luke xiv. 11.   [4] Ps. cxxx. 1, 2.

Wherefore, brethren, if we wish to attain to the summit
of humility and desire to arrive speedily at that heavenly
exaltation to which we ascend by the humility of the present
life, then must we set up a ladder of our ascending actions
like unto that which Jacob saw in his vision, whereon angels
appeared to him, descending and ascending. By that descent
and ascent we must surely understand nothing else than this,
that we descend by self-exaltation and ascend by humility.
And the ladder erected is our life in this world, which for
the humble of heart is raised up by the Lord unto heaven.
Now the sides of this ladder are our body and soul, into
which sides our divine vocation has fitted various degrees of
humility and discipline which we have to climb.

Jan. 26
May 27
Sept. 26

The first degree of humility, then, is that a man keep the
fear of God before his eyes, altogether shunning forgetful-
ness. Let him ever remember all the commandments of God,
and how hell will burn for their sins those that despise him;
and let him constantly turn over in his heart the eternal life
which is prepared for those that fear him. And guarding
himself always from sins and vices, whether of thought,
word, hand, foot, or self-will, and checking also the desires
of the flesh, let him consider that God is always beholding
him from heaven, that his actions are everywhere visible to
the eye of the Godhead, and are constantly being reported
to God by the angels. The prophet teaches us this when he
represents God as always present in our thoughts: *God
searcheth the heart and the reins*;[1] and again: *The Lord knoweth
the thoughts of men*;[2] and again he saith: *Thou hast understood my
thoughts from afar*;[3] and: *The thought of man shall praise thee*.[4]
In order then that he may be careful regarding his wrongful

Jan. 27
May 28
Sept. 27

[1] Ps. vii. 10. [2] Ps. xciii. 11. [3] Ps. cxxxviii. 3. [4] Ps. lxxv. 11.

thoughts, let the good brother say constantly in his heart:
*Then shall I be spotless before him, if I shall have kept myself from
my iniquity.*[1]

Jan. 28   We are, indeed, forbidden to do our own will by Scrip-
May 29 ture, which saith to us: *Turn away from thine own will.*[2] More-
Sept.28 over, we ask God in prayer that his will be done in us.

And rightly are we taught not to do our own will, since
we dread that sentence of Scripture: *There are ways which to
men seem right, but the ends thereof lead to the depths of hell*;[3] and
since we fear also what is said of the careless: *They are corrupt
and have become abominable in their pleasures.*[4] And in regard
to the desires of the flesh, let us believe that God is always
present to us, since the prophet says to the Lord: *All my
desire is before thee.*[5]

Jan. 29   We must be on our guard, then, against evil desires, for
May 30 death lies close by the gate of delight; whence Scripture
Sept.29 gives this command: *Go not after thy lusts.*[6] So if *the eyes of
the Lord behold the good and the evil,*[7] and the Lord is ever
*looking down from heaven upon the children of men, to see if there
be one soul that reflects and seeks God*;[8] and if our deeds are daily,
day and night, reported to the Lord by the angels assigned to
us: then, brethren, must we constantly beware, as the
prophet says in the psalm, lest God some day behold us fall-
ing into evil ways and turned unprofitable, and spare us for
this present time, because he is merciful and awaits our
amendment, but should say to us in the future: *These things
didst thou do, and I was silent.*[9]

[1] Ps. xvii. 24.   [2] Ecclus. xviii. 30.   [3] Prov. xvi. 25.   [4] Ps. xiii. 1.
[5] Ps. xxxvii. 10.   [6] Ecclus. xviii. 30.   [7] Prov. xv. 4.   [8] Ps. xiii. 2, 3.
[9] Ps. xlix. 21.

The second degree of humility is that a man love not his own will, nor delight in fulfilling his own desires, but carry out in deed the saying of the Lord: *I came not to do my own will, but the will of him who sent me.*[1] It is written also: *Self-will hath its punishment, but necessity winneth a crown.*

Jan. 30
May 31
Sept. 30

The third degree of humility is that a man for the love of God subject himself to his superior in all obedience, imitating the Lord, of whom the apostle says: *He was made obedient even unto death.*[2]

Jan. 31
June 1
Oct. 1

The fourth degree of humility is that, meeting in this obedience with difficulties and contradictions and even injustice, he should with a quiet mind hold fast to patience, and enduring neither tire nor run away; for the Scripture saith: *He that shall persevere to the end shall be saved;*[3] and again: *Let thy heart take courage, and wait thou for the Lord.*[4] And showing how the true disciple ought to endure all things, however contrary, for the Lord, it saith in the person of sufferers: *For thy sake we face death at every moment. We are reckoned no better than sheep marked down for slaughter.*[5] Then, confident in their hope of the divine reward, they go on with joy to declare: *But in all these things we overcome, through him that hath loved us.*[6] And again in another place the Scripture saith: *Thou, O God, hast put us to the proof: thou hast tested us as men test silver in the fire. Thou hast led us into a snare: thou hast bowed our backs with trouble.*[7] And to show that we ought to be under a superior, it goeth on to say: *Thou hast set men over our heads.*[8] Moreover, in adversities and injuries they patiently fulfil the Lord's commands: when struck on one

Feb. 1
June 2
Oct. 2

---

[1] John vi. 38. [2] Phil. ii. 8. [3] Mat. x. 22. [4] Ps. xxvi. 14.
[5] Rom. viii. 36. [6] Ibid. 37. [7] Ps. lxv. 10, 11. [8] Ibid. 12.

cheek they offer the other, when robbed of their tunic they surrender also their cloak, when forced to go a mile they go two, with the apostle Paul they bear with false brethren, and they bless those that curse them.

Feb. 2
June 3
Oct. 3

The fifth degree of humility is that he humbly confess and conceal not from his abbot any evil thoughts that enter his heart, and any secret sins that he has committed. To this does Scripture exhort us, saying: *Make known thy way unto the Lord and hope in him.*[1] And again: *Confess to the Lord, for he is good, and his mercy endureth for ever.*[2] And further: *I have made known my sin to thee, and my faults I have not concealed. I said: I will be my own accuser and confess my faults to the Lord, and with that thou didst remit the guilt of my sin.*[3]

Feb. 3
June 4
Oct. 4

The sixth degree of humility is that a monk be content with the meanest and worst of everything, and esteem himself, in regard to the work that is given him, as a bad and unworthy workman, saying to himself with the prophet: *I am brought to nothing; I am all ignorance; I am become as a dumb beast before thee; yet am I ever close to thee.*[4]

Feb. 4
June 5
Oct. 5

The seventh degree of humility is that he should not only in his speech declare himself lower and of less account than all others, but should in his own inmost heart believe it, humbling himself and saying with the prophet: *But I am a worm and no man, a byword to all men and the laughing-stock of the people.*[5] *I have been lifted up only to be humbled and confounded;*[6] and again: *It is good for me that thou hast humbled me, that I may learn thy commandments.*[7]

[1] Ps. xxxvi. 5.   [2] Ps. cv. 1.   [3] Ps. xxxi. 5.   [4] Ps. lxxii. 22, 23.
[5] Ps. xxi. 7.   [6] Ps. lxxxvii. 16.   [7] Ps. cxviii. 71.

The eighth degree of humility is that a monk do nothing except what is commended by the common rule of the monastery and the example of his superiors.

Feb. 5
June 6
Oct. 6

The ninth degree of humility is that a monk restrain his tongue and keep silence, not speaking until he is questioned. For Scripture showeth that *in much talking thou canst not avoid sin*;[1] and that *the talkative man shall not prosper on the earth.*[2]

Feb. 6
June 7
Oct. 7

The tenth degree of humility is that he be not ready and prompt to laughter, for it is written: *The fool lifteth up his voice in laughter.*[3]

Feb. 7
June 8
Oct. 8

The eleventh degree of humility is that a monk, when he speaks, do so gently and without laughter, humbly and seriously, in few and sensible words, and without clamour. It is written: *A wise man is known by the fewness of his words.*[4]

Feb. 8
June 9
Oct. 9

The twelfth degree of humility is that a monk should not only be humble of heart, but should also in his behaviour always manifest his humility to those who look upon him. That is to say, that whether he is at the Work of God, in the oratory, in the monastery, in the garden, on the road, in the fields, or anywhere else, and whether sitting, walking, or standing, he should always have his head bowed and his eyes downcast, pondering always the guilt of his sins, and considering that he is about to be brought before the dread judgement seat of God. Let him constantly say in his heart

Feb. 9
June 10
Oct. 10

[1] Prov. x. 19.   [2] Ps. cxxxix. 12.   [3] Ecclus. xxi. 23.
[4] From the 'Sentences of Sextus', a collection of pithy sayings, made by a Greek philosopher and latinized by Rufinus.

what was said with downcast eyes by the publican in the Gospel: *Lord, I a sinner am not worthy to raise mine eyes to heaven*;[1] and again with the prophet: *I am bowed down and humbled on every side*.[2]

Then, when all these degrees of humility have been climbed, the monk will presently come to that perfect love of God which casts out all fear; whereby he will begin to observe without labour, as though naturally and by habit, all those precepts which formerly he did not observe without fear: no longer for fear of hell, but for love of Christ and through good habit and delight in virtue. And this will the Lord deign to show forth by the power of his Spirit in his workman now cleansed from vice and from sin.

CHAPTER

8

THE DIVINE OFFICE
AT NIGHT

Feb. 10
June 11
Oct. 11

IN winter, that is from the first of November until Easter, prudence dictates that the brethren shall rise at the eighth hour of the night, so that their sleep may extend for a moderate space beyond midnight, and they may rise with digestion completed. Those brethren, who need a better knowledge of them, should devote the time that remains after Matins to the study of the psalms and lessons. From Easter to the aforesaid first of November, let the hour of rising be so arranged that there be a very short interval after Matins, in which the brethren may go out for the necessities of nature, to be followed at once by Lauds, which should be said at dawn.

[1] Luke xviii. 13 (in substance).   [2] Ps. cxviii. 107.

CHAPTER
9

HOW MANY PSALMS
ARE TO BE SAID AT
THE NIGHT OFFICE

IN the aforesaid winter season, there is first the versicle *Domine labia mea aperies, et os meum annuntiabit laudem tuam*,[1] to be said three times; then must follow the third psalm and the *Gloria*; then the ninety-fourth psalm to be chanted with an antiphon, or at any rate to be chanted. Let the hymn follow next, and then six psalms with antiphons. When these are finished and the versicle said, let the abbot give a blessing; and then, all being seated in their places, let three lessons be read from the book on the lectern by the brethren in their turns, and let three responsories be chanted between them. Two of the responsories shall be said without the *Gloria*; but after the third lesson let the reader chant the *Gloria*. And as soon as he has begun it, let all rise from their seats in honour and reverence to the Holy Trinity. The books to be read at Matins shall be the inspired Scriptures of the Old and New Testaments, and also the commentaries on them which have been made by well-known and orthodox Catholic Fathers. After these three lessons with their responsories, let there follow the remaining six psalms, which shall be chanted with *Alleluia*. After these shall follow the lesson from the apostle, to be recited by heart, the versicle, and the petition of the litany, that is *Kyrie eleison*. And so shall the Night Office end.

Feb. 11
June 12
Oct. 12

[1] Ps. l. 17.

CHAPTER

IO

HOW THE NIGHT OFFICE IS TO BE SAID IN SUMMER

Feb. 12
June 13
Oct. 13

FROM Easter to the first of November, let the number of the psalms be exactly as given above; but let there be this difference, that the lessons from the book be not read, on account of the shortness of the nights. Instead of the three lessons, let there be but one from the Old Testament, said by heart, and let it be followed by a short responsory. But all else should be done as has been said; that is to say that there should never be less than twelve psalms at the Night Office, not counting the third and ninety-fourth.

CHAPTER

II

HOW THE NIGHT OFFICE IS TO BE SAID ON SUNDAYS

Feb. 13
June 14
Oct. 14

ON Sundays let the brethren rise earlier for the Night Office, in which let this order be kept. When the six psalms and the versicle have been chanted, as we ordained above, and all are seated in their stalls, duly and in order, then let there be read from the book, as we said before, four lessons with their responsories. In the fourth responsory only shall the reader chant the *Gloria*, and when he begins it let all rise immediately with reverence. After these lessons let there follow in order another six psalms with antiphons, like the previous ones, and a versicle. After these again let four more lessons be read with their responsories, in the same way as before. After these let there be three canticles from the book of the prophets, as appointed by the abbot, and let these canticles be chanted with *Alleluia*. Then, when the versicle has been said and the abbot has given the blessing, let another four lessons be read from the New Testament, in the same way as before. When the fourth responsory is finished, let the abbot begin the hymn *Te Deum laudamus*. When that has been said, the abbot shall read the lesson from the book of the Gospels, all standing with fear and reverence. That having been read, let all answer *Amen*, and then let the abbot follow with the hymn *Te decet laus*, and the blessing having been given let them begin Lauds. This order of Matins shall be observed on Sundays all the year round, both in summer and winter; unless (which God forbid) they be late in rising, so that the lessons and responsories have to be shortened. However, let the greatest care be taken that this do not happen; but if it happen, let him through whose neglect it has occurred, make due satisfaction to God in the oratory.

CHAPTER

12

**HOW THE OFFICE
OF LAUDS IS
TO BE SAID**

LAUDS on Sundays should begin with the sixty-sixth psalm chanted straight through without an antiphon. After that let the fiftieth psalm be said, with *Alleluia*; then the hundred and seventeenth and the sixty-second; then the *Benedicite* and the *Laudate* psalms; then a lesson from the Apocalypse to be recited by heart, the responsory, the hymn, the versicle, the canticle from the Gospel book, the *Kyrie eleison*, and so the end.

Feb. 14
June 15
Oct. 15

CHAPTER

13

HOW LAUDS SHALL
BE SAID ON
ORDINARY DAYS

Feb. 15
June 16
Oct. 16

ON ordinary days Lauds shall be celebrated in the following manner: let the sixty-sixth psalm be said without an antiphon and somewhat slowly, as on Sunday, in order that all may assemble in time for the fiftieth, which should be said with an antiphon. After this let two other psalms be said according to custom: that is, on Monday the fifth and thirty-fifth; on Tuesday the forty-second and fifty-sixth; on Wednesday the sixty-third and sixty-fourth; on Thursday the eighty-seventh and eighty-ninth; on Friday the seventy-fifth and ninety-first; and on Saturday the hundred and forty-second and the canticle from Deuteronomy, which must be divided into two parts. But on the other days let there be a canticle from the prophets, each on its own day, according to the custom of the Roman church. After that let the *Laudate* psalms follow; then a lesson from the apostle to be said by heart, the responsory, the hymn, the versicle, the canticle from the Gospels, the *Kyrie eleison*, and so the end.

Feb. 16
June 17
Oct. 17

Of course, the Offices of Lauds and Vespers shall never be allowed to end without the superior finally reciting, in the hearing of all, the whole of the Lord's Prayer. The purpose of this is the removal of those thorns of scandal, or mutual offence, which are wont to arise in communities. For, being warned by the covenant which they make in that prayer, when they say *Forgive us as we forgive*, the brethren will cleanse their souls of such faults. At the other Offices, however, only the last part of that prayer shall be said aloud, so that all may answer *Sed libera nos a malo.*

CHAPTER
14

HOW THE NIGHT OFFICE
IS TO BE PERFORMED
ON SAINTS' DAYS

O N the feasts of Saints and on all festivals, let the
Office be performed as we have prescribed for
Sundays, except that the psalms, antiphons, and
lessons belonging to the particular day are to be said; but
the general arrangement of the Office shall be as laid down
above.

Feb. 17
June 18
Oct. 18

CHAPTER
15

AT WHAT SEASONS
ALLELUIA IS
TO BE SAID

F ROM the sacred feast of Easter until Pentecost, let
Alleluia be said always both with the psalms and with
the responsories. From Pentecost until the beginning
of Lent, let it be said every night at Matins with the second
six psalms only. On every Sunday out of Lent, let *Alleluia* be
said with the canticles of Matins, and with the psalms of
Lauds, Prime, Terce, Sext, and None; but let Vespers then
have an antiphon. The responsories are never to be said with
Alleluia, except from Easter to Pentecost.

Feb. 18
June 19
Oct. 19

<table>
<tr><td>CHAPTER</td><td>HOW THE WORK OF GOD</td></tr>
<tr><td>16</td><td>IS TO BE PERFORMED
IN THE DAY-TIME</td></tr>
</table>

Feb. 19
June 20
Oct. 20

THE prophet saith: *Seven times a day have I given praise to thee.*[1] We shall observe this sacred number of seven, if we fulfil the duties of our service in the Hours of Lauds, Prime, Terce, Sext, None, Vespers, and Compline; for it was of these Day Hours that he said: *Seven times a day have I given praise to thee.*[1] But of the Night Office the same prophet saith: *At midnight I rose to give praise to thee.*[2] At these times, therefore, let us render praise to our Creator *for the judgements of his justice*:[1] that is, at Lauds, Prime, Terce, Sext, None, Vespers, and Compline; and let us rise in the night to praise him.

<table>
<tr><td>CHAPTER</td><td>HOW MANY PSALMS</td></tr>
<tr><td>17</td><td>ARE TO BE SAID
AT THESE HOURS</td></tr>
</table>

Feb. 20
June 21
Oct. 21

WE have already settled the psalmody of Matins and Lauds; let us now look to the remaining Hours. At Prime let three psalms be said, one by one and not under the same *Gloria*; and before the psalms begin, but after the verse *Deus in adjutorium*, the hymn proper to that Hour. Then, at the end of the three psalms, let there be the lesson, versicle, *Kyrie eleison*, and concluding prayers. The Offices of Terce, Sext, and None are to be performed in the same way: that is, *Deus in adjutorium*, proper hymn, three psalms, lesson, versicle, *Kyrie eleison*, and concluding prayers. If the community be a large one, let the psalms be sung with

[1] Ps. cxviii. 164. [2] Ibid. 62.

antiphons; but if small, let them be sung straightforward.

Let the service of Vespers consist of four psalms with antiphons. After these psalms let a lesson be recited; and then the responsory, hymn, versicle, canticle from the Gospels, *Kyrie eleison*, and the Lord's Prayer to conclude. Let Compline be limited to the saying of three psalms, and these said straightforward without an antiphon. After the psalms let there be the hymn for that Hour, the lesson, versicle, *Kyrie eleison*, and the blessing to conclude.

CHAPTER

18

IN WHAT ORDER
THE PSALMS ARE
TO BE SAID

Fɪʀsᴛ let there be said the verse: *Deus in adjutorium meum intende, Domine ad adjuvandum me festina*,[1] and *Gloria*; then the hymn proper to each Hour. Then at Prime on Sunday, four sections of the hundred and eighteenth psalm; and at each of the remaining hours, that is Terce, Sext, and None, three sections of the same hundred and eighteenth psalm. At Prime on Monday let three psalms be said, namely the first, second, and sixth. And so at Prime every day until Sunday let there be said three psalms taken in their order up to the nineteenth; but let the ninth and seventeenth be each divided into two. Thus it comes about that the Night Office on Sundays will always begin with the twentieth psalm.

Feb. 21
June 22
Oct. 22

[1] Ps. lxix. 1.

At Terce, Sext, and None on Monday, let the remaining nine sections of the hundred and eighteenth psalm be said, three at each of these Hours. The hundred and eighteenth psalm having been said thus on two days, that is Sunday and Monday, let Terce, Sext, and None of Tuesday each have three psalms, taken in order from the hundred and nineteenth to the hundred and twenty-seventh, i.e. nine psalms. And let these psalms be repeated at these Hours every day until Sunday; but let the arrangement of hymns, lessons, and versicles be kept the same on all days. Thus Prime on Sunday will always begin with the hundred and eighteenth psalm.

Vespers shall be sung every day with four psalms. Let these begin with the hundred and ninth and go on to the hundred and forty-seventh, those being omitted which are set aside for special Hours, namely, the hundred and seventeenth to the hundred and twenty-seventh, the hundred and thirty-third and the hundred and forty-second. All the rest are to be said at Vespers. And since there are three psalms too few, let the longer psalms in the above number be divided, namely, the hundred and thirty-eighth, the hundred and forty-third, and the hundred and forty-fourth. But the hundred and sixteenth psalm, being short, shall be joined to the hundred and fifteenth. The order of the vesper psalms being thus settled, let the rest of the Hour, that is to say, lesson, responsory, hymn, versicle, and canticle, be carried out as we prescribed before. At Compline let the same psalms be repeated every day: that is, the fourth, the ninetieth, and the hundred and thirty-third.

The order of psalms for the Day Hours being thus ar- (Feb. 24
ranged, let all the remaining psalms be equally distributed in L.Y.)
among the seven Night Offices, by dividing the longer psalms June 25
and assigning twelve psalms to each night. But we strongly Oct. 25
recommend, if this arrangement of the psalms be displeasing
to anyone, that he arrange them otherwise, as shall seem
better to him; provided always that he take care that the
psalter with its full hundred and fifty psalms be chanted
every week and begun afresh every Sunday at Matins. For
those monks show themselves very slothful in their sacred
service, who in the course of the week sing less than the
psalter and the customary canticles, whereas we read that
our holy fathers strenuously fulfilled in a single day what I
pray that we lukewarm monks may perform in a whole
week.

CHAPTER
19
THE MANNER OF SAYING
THE DIVINE OFFICE

WE believe that God is present everywhere and that   Feb. 24
the eyes of the Lord in every place behold the good and the   (or 25)
evil;[1] but let us especially believe this without any June 26
doubting when we are performing the Divine Office. There-   Oct. 26
fore, let us ever remember the words of the prophet: *Serve
ye the Lord in fear*;[2] and again, *Sing ye wisely*;[3] and, *In the sight
of the angels will I sing to thee.*[4] Let us then consider how we

[1] Prov. xv. 3.   [2] Ps. ii. 11.   [3] Ps. xlvi. 8.   [4] Ps. cxxxvii. 2.

ought to behave ourselves in the presence of God and his angels, and so sing the psalms that mind and voice may be in harmony.

CHAPTER

20

OF REVERENCE IN PRAYER

Feb. 25
(or 26)
June 27
Oct. 27

IF we wish to prefer a petition to men of high station, we do not presume to do it without humility and respect; how much more ought we to supplicate the Lord God of all things with all humility and pure devotion. And let us be sure that we shall not be heard for our much speaking, but for purity of heart and tears of compunction. Our prayer, therefore, ought to be short and pure, unless it chance to be prolonged by the impulse and inspiration of divine grace. In community, however, let prayer be very short, and when the superior has given the signal let all rise together.

CHAPTER

21

THE DEANS OF THE MONASTERY

Feb. 26
(or 27)
June 28
Oct. 28

IF the community be a large one, let there be chosen out of it brethren of good repute and observant life, and let them be appointed deans. They shall take charge of their deaneries in all things, observing the commandments of God and the instructions of their abbot. And let such men be chosen as deans that the abbot may without anxiety share his burdens among them; and let them not be chosen by order, but according to their worthiness of life, learning, and wisdom. Should any of these deans become puffed up with pride and be found worthy of censure, let him be corrected once, and a second, and a third time; if he will not amend, then let him be deposed from his office and another, who is worthy of it, put in his place. And we order the same to be done in the case of the prior.

CHAPTER

22

HOW THE
MONKS ARE
TO SLEEP

Let them sleep each one in a separate bed. Let their beds be assigned to them in accordance with the date of their conversion, subject to the abbot's dispositions. If it be possible, let them all sleep in one place; but if their numbers do not allow of this, let them sleep by tens or twenties, with seniors to supervise them. There shall be a light burning in the dormitory throughout the night. Let them sleep clothed and girt with girdles or cords, *but not with their belts*, so that they may not have their knives at their sides while they are sleeping, and be cut by them in their sleep. Being clothed they will thus always be ready, and rising at the signal without any delay may hasten to forestall one another to the Work of God; yet this with all gravity and self-restraint. The younger brethren shall not have their beds by themselves, but shall be mixed with the seniors. When they rise for the Work of God, let them gently encourage one another, on account of the excuses to which the sleepy are addicted.

Feb. 27
(or 28)
June 29
Oct. 29

CHAPTER

23

OF EXCOMMUNICATION FOR FAULTS

Feb. 28
(or 29)
June 30
Oct. 30

IF any brother shall be found contumacious, or dis-obedient, or proud, or a murmurer, or in any way despising and contravening the holy Rule and the orders of his superiors: let such a one, according to our Lord's commandment, be admonished secretly by his superiors for a first and a second time. If he do not amend, let him be rebuked publicly before all. But if even then he do not correct his life, let him suffer excommunication, provided that he understands the gravity of that penalty. If, however, he be perverse, let him undergo corporal punishment.

CHAPTER

24

WHAT THE MEASURE OF EXCOMMUNICATION SHOULD BE

Mar. 1
July 1
Oct. 31

THE measure of excommunication and punishment should be proportioned to the gravity of the fault, which shall be determined by the abbot. If a brother be found guilty of a lesser fault, let him be excluded from sharing the common table. And this shall be the rule for one who is thus excluded from the common table: Until he have made satisfaction, he shall not intone psalm or antiphon in the oratory, nor read a lesson; and he shall have his meals alone, after the community meals. If the brethren, for instance, eat at the sixth hour, let him eat at the ninth; if they eat at the ninth hour, let him eat in the evening; until by suitable satisfaction he have obtained pardon.

CHAPTER
25

OF GRAVER
FAULTS

THE brother who is guilty of a graver fault shall be
excluded both from the table and from the oratory.
Let none of the brethren consort with him or speak to
him. Let him work alone at the task enjoined him and abide
in penitential sorrow, pondering that terrible sentence of
the apostle: *Such a one is delivered to Satan for the destruction of
the flesh, that the spirit may be saved in the day of our Lord.*[1] Let
him take his meals alone, in the measure and at the hour
which the abbot shall consider suitable for him. He shall
not be blessed by any passer-by, nor the food which is given
him.

Mar. 2
July 2
Nov. 1

CHAPTER
26

OF THOSE WHO WITHOUT
LEAVE CONSORT WITH
THE EXCOMMUNICATED

IF any brother presume, without the abbot's leave, to
consort in any way with an excommunicated brother,
or to converse with him, or to send him a message, let
him receive the like punishment of excommunication.

Mar. 3
July 3
Nov. 2

[1] 1 Cor. v. 5.

CHAPTER

27

THAT THE ABBOT BE SOLICITOUS FOR THE EXCOMMUNICATED

Mar. 4
July 4
Nov. 3

LET the abbot exercise all diligence in his care for err-ing brethren, for *they that are in health need not a physician, but they that are sick*.[1] He ought, therefore, as a wise physician, to use every remedy in his power. Let him send *senpectae*, that is old and prudent brethren, who may as it were secretly comfort the troubled brother, in-ducing him to make humble satisfaction and consoling him *lest he be swallowed up with overmuch sorrow*.[2] As the apostle also saith: *Let charity be strengthened towards him*;[3] and let everyone pray for him.

For the abbot is bound to use the greatest care, and to exercise all prudence and diligence, so that he may not lose any of the sheep entrusted to him. Let him know that what he has undertaken is the charge of weakly souls, and not a tyranny over the strong; and let him fear the threat of the prophet, wherein God saith: *What you saw to be fat, that ye took to yourselves: and what was feeble, ye cast away*.[4] And let him imitate the merciful example of the Good Shepherd, who left the ninety and nine sheep in the moun-tains and went after the one sheep that had strayed; and had so great pity on its weakness, that he deigned to place it on his own sacred shoulders and so bring it back to the flock.[5]

---

[1] Mat. ix. 12.   [2] 2 Cor. ii. 7.   [3] Ibid.   [4] *Cf.* Ezech. xxxiv. 3, 4.
[5] *Cf.* Luke xv. 4, 5.

CHAPTER
28

OF THOSE WHO THOUGH OFTEN CORRECTED WILL NOT AMEND

I F any brother, though often corrected for some offence and even excommunicated, do not amend, let him receive more severe correction; that is to say, let the punishment of the rod be administered to him. But if even so he do not amend, or perchance (which God forbid) being puffed up with pride would even defend his deeds, then let the abbot follow the procedure of a prudent physician. Having applied the fomentations and ointments of his exhortations, having used the medicine of the Holy Scriptures and last of all the cautery of excommunication and the strokes of the rod: then, if he see that all his trouble is of no avail, let him employ a greater thing still, namely the prayers of himself and all the brethren, that God, who can do all things, may effect the cure of the sick brother.

Mar. 5
July 5
Nov. 4

But if he be not healed even in this way, then let the abbot use the knife of amputation, as the apostle saith: *Banish the offender from your company*;[1] and again: *If the unbeliever depart, let him depart*;[2] lest one diseased sheep contaminate the whole flock.

CHAPTER
29

WHETHER BRETHREN WHO LEAVE THE MONASTERY SHOULD BE RECEIVED AGAIN

A BROTHER who by his own fault leaves the monastery, should, if he wish to return, first promise full amendment for his having gone away; and then let him be received back again in the lowest place, in order that

Mar. 6
July 6
Nov. 5

[1] 1 Cor. v. 13. [2] 1 Cor. vii. 15.

37

his humility may thus be tested. Should he depart again, let him be received back again, and so a third time; but after that he should understand that all prospect of return is denied him.

<table>
<tr><td>CHAPTER
30</td><td>HOW BOYS
ARE TO BE
CORRECTED</td></tr>
</table>

Mar. 7
July 7
Nov. 6

EVERY age and degree of understanding should have its appropriate measure of discipline. Therefore, as often as faults are committed by boys, or by youths, or by those who do not understand the greatness of the penalty of excommunication, let such offenders be punished with severe fasts or chastised with sharp stripes, in order that they may be cured.

<table>
<tr><td>CHAPTER
31</td><td>WHAT KIND OF MAN
THE CELLARER OF THE
MONASTERY SHOULD BE</td></tr>
</table>

Mar. 8
July 8
Nov. 7

As cellarer of the monastery let there be chosen out of the community a man who is prudent, of mature character, temperate, not a great eater, not proud, not headstrong, not rough-spoken, not lazy, not wasteful, but a God-fearing man who may be like a father to the whole community. Let him have charge of everything; let him do nothing without the abbot's orders, but keep to his instructions. Let him not vex the brethren. If any brother happen to make an unreasonable demand, he should not vex him with a contemptuous denial, but reasonably and humbly refuse the improper request. Let him keep guard over his own soul, remembering always the saying of the apostle that *he that hath served well, secures for himself a good standing*.[1] Let him take the greatest care of the sick, of children, of guests, and of the poor, knowing without doubt that he will have to render an account for all these on the Day of Judgement. Let him look upon all the utensils of the monastery and its whole property as upon the sacred vessels of the altar. Let him not think that anything may be neglected. Let him neither practise avarice, nor be wasteful and a squanderer of the monastery's substance; but let him do all things with measure and in accordance with the instructions of the abbot.

Above all things let him have humility, and if he have nothing else to give, let him give a good word in answer; for it is written: *A good word is above the best gift*.[2] Let him have under his care all those things which the abbot has assigned to him, but presume not to deal with what he has forbidden to him. Let him give the brethren their appointed allowance of food without any arrogance or delay, that they may not be scandalized, mindful of what the Scripture saith that he deserves *who shall scandalize one of these little ones*.[3] If the community be a large one, let helpers be given him, so that by their assistance he may fulfil with a quiet mind the charge that has been committed to him. Let those things which have to be asked for and those things which have to be given, be asked for and given at the proper times; so that no one may be troubled or vexed in the house of God.

Mar. 9
July 9
Nov. 8

[1] 1 Tim. iii. 13.   [2] Ecclus. xviii. 17.   [3] Mat. xviii. 6.

THE TOOLS AND PROPERTY OF THE MONASTERY

FOR the care of the monastery's property in tools, clothing, and all other articles, let the abbot appoint brethren on whose life and character he can rely; and let him, as he shall judge fit, commit the various articles to them, to be looked after and to be collected again. Let the abbot keep a list of them, so that when the brethren succeed one another in their offices, he may know what he is giving out and what receiving back. If anyone treat the property of the monastery in a slovenly or careless manner, let him be corrected; if he do not amend, let him undergo the punishment of the Rule.

WHETHER MONKS SHOULD HAVE ANYTHING OF THEIR OWN

THIS vice especially ought to be utterly rooted out of the monastery. Let no one presume to give or receive anything without the abbot's leave, or to have anything as his own, anything whatever, whether book or tablets or pen or whatever it may be; for monks should not have even their bodies and wills at their own disposal. But let them look to the father of the monastery for all that they require, and let it be unlawful to have anything which the abbot has not given or allowed. And, as the Scripture saith, *let all things be common to all, nor let anyone say that anything is his own*[1] or claim it for himself. But if anyone shall be

[1] *Cf.* Acts iv. 32.

40

found to indulge in this most wicked vice, let him be admonished once and a second time; if he do not amend, let him undergo punishment.

CHAPTER

34

WHETHER ALL SHOULD
RECEIVE NECESSARIES
IN LIKE MEASURE

LET us follow the Scripture: *Distribution was made to every man according as he had need.*[1] By this we do not mean that there should be respect of persons (God forbid), but consideration for infirmities. He that needeth less, let him thank God and not be discontented; he that needeth more, let him be humbled for his infirmity and not made proud by the mercy shown to him: so will all the members be at peace. Above all, let not the vice of murmuring show itself in any word or sign, for any reason whatever. But if a brother be found guilty of it, let him undergo strict punishment.

Mar. 12
July 12
Nov. 11

CHAPTER

35

OF THE WEEKLY
KITCHENERS

LET the brethren serve one another, and let no one be excused from the kitchen service, unless for sickness or because he is occupied in some business of importance. For this service brings increase of reward and of charity. But let the weak have help provided for them, that they may not perform their office with sadness; and indeed

Mar. 13
July 13
Nov. 12

[1] Acts iv. 35.

let everyone have help, according to the size of the community or the circumstances of the locality. If the community be a large one, let the cellarer be excused from the kitchen service; and so also those who are occupied in any important business, as we said before. Let the rest serve one another in charity. When the server is ending his week on the Saturday, let him do the washing. He shall wash the towels which the brethren use for drying their hands and feet; and both the servers, that is, the server who is ending his week and he who is about to begin, shall wash the feet of the whole community. Let the outgoing server restore the vessels of his office to the cellarer clean and sound; and let the cellarer then deliver them to the incoming server, in order that he may know what he is giving out and what receiving back.

Mar. 14
July 14
Nov. 13

Let the weekly servers, an hour before the meal, receive each of them, over and above the regular allowance, a drink and some bread, in order that at the meal time they may serve their brethren without murmuring and undue hardship; but on feast days they must wait until after Mass. On Sunday, immediately after Lauds, the incoming and outgoing servers shall prostrate themselves before all the brethren in the oratory and ask for their prayers. Let the server who is ending his week say this verse: *Benedictus es Domine Deus, qui adjuvasti me et consolatus es me.*[1] When this has been said three times and the outgoing server has received his blessing, then let the incoming server follow and say: *Deus in adjutorium meum intende, Domine ad adjuvandum me festina.*[2] Let this too be repeated thrice by all the brethren, and having received his blessing let him enter on his week.

---

[1] Dan. iii. 26; Ps. lxxxv. 17.   [2] Ps. lxix. 1.

CHAPTER

36

OF SICK
BRETHREN

BEFORE all things and above all things care must be taken of the sick, so that they may be served in very deed as Christ himself; for he said: *I was sick and ye visited me;*[1] and, *what ye did to one of these least ones, ye did unto me.*[2] But let the sick on their part consider that they are being served for the honour of God, and not provoke their brethren who are serving them by their unreasonable demands. Yet they should be patiently borne with, because from such as these is gained a more abundant reward. Therefore let the abbot take the greatest care that they suffer no neglect. For these sick brethren let there be assigned a special room and an attendant who is God-fearing, diligent, and careful. Let the use of baths be afforded to the sick as often as may be expedient; but to the healthy, and especially to the young, let them be granted seldom. Moreover, let the use of fleshmeat be granted to the sick who are very weak, for the restoration of their strength; but, as soon as they are better, let all abstain from fleshmeat as usual. Let the abbot take the greatest care that the sick be not neglected by the cellarers and attendants; for he must answer for all the misdeeds of his disciples.

[1] Mat. xxv. 36.   [2] Ibid. 40.

CHAPTER

37

OF OLD MEN AND CHILDREN

ALTHOUGH human nature itself is drawn to pity towards these times of life, that is, towards old men and children, yet let them be provided for also by the authority of the Rule. Let there be constant consideration for their weakness, and on no account let the rigour of the Rule in regard to food be applied to them. Let them, on the contrary, receive compassionate consideration and take their meals before the regular hours.

CHAPTER

38

OF THE WEEKLY READER

AT the meals of the brethren there should not fail to be reading; nor should the reader be anyone who may chance to take up the book; but let there be a reader for the whole week who shall enter upon his office on Sunday. Let this incoming reader, after Mass and Communion, ask all to pray for him that God may preserve him from the spirit of pride. He shall intone three times in the oratory the versicle: *Domine, labia mea aperies, et os meum annuntiabit laudem tuam,*[1] which shall each time be repeated after him by the choir. And so, having received his blessing, let him enter upon his reading. And let there be the greatest silence, so that no whisper, and no voice but the reader's, may be heard there. But for the things that they need as they eat and drink, let the brethren so supply them to one another

[1] Ps. l. 17.

that no one shall need to ask for anything. If, however, there be any need, then let the thing be asked for by means of some sign rather than by speech. Nor let anyone venture there to ask questions about the reading or anything else, lest it give occasion for disorder. However, the superior, if he thinks fit, may say a few words for the edification of the brethren. Let the weekly reader be given a little bread and wine before he begins to read, on account of the Holy Communion and lest the fast might be hard for him to bear. Let him have his meal afterwards with the kitcheners and servers of the week. The brethren are not to read or sing each in his turn, but those only who give edification to the hearers.

CHAPTER
39

THE MEASURE
OF FOOD

W E believe it to be sufficient for the daily meal, whether that be at the sixth or the ninth hour, that every table should have two cooked dishes, on account of individual infirmities, so that he who perchance cannot eat of the one, may make his meal of the other. Therefore, let two cooked dishes suffice for all the brethren; and if any fruit or young vegetables are available, let a third be added. Let a good pound weight of bread suffice for the day, whether there be one meal only, or both dinner and supper. If they are to have supper, let a third part of the pound be reserved by the cellarer, to be given to them for their supper. But if their work chance to be heavier, the abbot shall have the choice and power, should it be expedient, to increase this allowance. Above all things, however,

Mar. 18
July 18
Nov. 17

gluttony must be avoided, so that a monk never be surprised by a surfeit; for there is nothing so unfitting for a christian as surfeiting, according to our Lord's words: *Take heed lest your hearts be overcharged with surfeiting*.[1] Young boys shall not receive the same amount of food as their elders, but less; and frugality shall be observed in all circumstances. Except the sick who are very weak, let all abstain entirely from the flesh of four-footed animals.

CHAPTER

40

THE MEASURE
OF DRINK

Mar. 19
July 19
Nov. 18

EVERY *man hath his proper gift from God, one after this manner, and another after that.*[2] It is therefore with some misgiving that we determine how much others should eat or drink. Nevertheless, keeping in view the needs of weaker brethren, we believe that a hemina of wine a day is sufficient for each. But those upon whom God bestows the gift of abstinence, should know that they shall have a special reward.

But if the circumstances of the place, or their work, or the heat of summer require more, let the superior be free to grant it. Yet let him always take care that neither surfeit nor drunkenness supervene. We do, indeed, read that wine is no drink for monks; but since nowadays monks cannot be persuaded of this, let us at least agree upon this, to drink temperately and not to satiety: for *wine maketh even the wise to fall away*.[3] But when the circumstances of the place are such that the aforesaid measure cannot be had, but much less or even none at all, then let the monks who dwell there bless

[1] Luke xxi. 34.   [2] 1 Cor. vii. 7.   [3] Ecclus. xix. 2.

God and not murmur. Above all things do we give this admonition, that they abstain from murmuring.

41

THE HOURS OF MEALS

FROM the feast of Easter until Pentecost let the brethren dine at the sixth hour and sup in the evening. From Pentecost throughout the summer, unless the monks have work in the fields or the heat of the summer oppress them, let them fast on Wednesdays and Fridays until the ninth hour; on the other days let them dine at the sixth hour. If they have field work or the summer heat be extreme, this dinner at the sixth hour shall be the daily practice, according to the abbot's discretion. And let him so arrange and ordain all things that souls may be saved and that the brethren may do their work without justifiable murmuring. From September the 14th[1] until the beginning of Lent let them always have their meal at the ninth hour. In Lent until Easter let them have it in the evening. Vespers, however, should be so timed that the brethren may not need lamplight at the meal, but that all may be accomplished by daylight. And at all times let the hour of the late meal or supper be so arranged that everything may be done by daylight.

Mar. 20
July 20
Nov. 19

[1] Which actually is the day after the Ides. See *Kalendas Octobres* (p. 110) and Note 72.

CHAPTER

42

THAT NO ONE SPEAK
AFTER COMPLINE

Mar. 21
July 21
Nov. 20

MONKS should practise silence at all times, but especially at night. This rule applies generally, whether the day be a fast day or a non-fasting day. On the latter, as soon as they have risen from supper, let them all sit together in one place, and let a brother read the Conferences of Cassian or the Lives of the Fathers, or something else that may edify the hearers; but not the Heptateuch or Kings, because it will not be good for weak minds to hear those parts of Scripture at that time of day; let those books be read at other times. On fast days, however, the aforesaid reading of the Conferences shall take place shortly after Vespers. As to that reading itself, let four or five pages be read, or as much as time permits. This period of reading will allow of the arrival of such brethren as may chance to be engaged in special duties.

And so, being all assembled in the one place, let them say Compline. And when they come out of Compline, let there be no further permission for anyone to say anything. Severe punishment shall be accorded to anyone who is found to infringe this rule of silence, unless speech be made necessary by the arrival of guests or the abbot give someone an order. But, even so, this speaking itself should be done with the utmost gravity and the most becoming restraint.

CHAPTER

43

OF THOSE WHO COME LATE TO THE WORK OF GOD OR TO TABLE

As soon as the signal for the Divine Office has been heard, let them abandon what they have in hand and assemble with the greatest speed, yet soberly, so that no occasion be given for levity. Let nothing, therefore, be put before the Work of God.

Mar. 22
July 22
Nov. 21

If anyone arrive at the Night Office after the *Gloria* of the ninety-fourth psalm, which we wish for this reason to be said very slowly and deliberately, let him not take his proper place in the choir, but stand last of all, or in the place apart which the abbot has appointed for such careless persons, so that they may be seen by him and by all, until at the completion of the Work of God he do penance by public satisfaction. The reason why we have ordained that they should stand in the last place or apart, is that being seen by all they may amend for very shame. For if they were to remain outside the oratory, there might be one who would go to bed again and sleep, or at least sit himself down outside and indulge in idle talk, and thus an occasion would be provided for the evil one. But let them enter the oratory, that they may not lose the whole Office and may amend for the future. At the Day Hours let him who does not arrive at the Work of God until after the Verse and the *Gloria* of the first psalm which follows it, stand in the last place, according to our ruling above, nor let him presume to join the choir until he have done penance, unless the abbot have pardoned him and given him permission. But, even so, the man guilty of this fault should do penance.

In the case of meals, if anyone do not arrive before the verse, so that all may say the verse and the prayers together and all at the same time go to the table—if anyone by his carelessness or fault do not arrive, he shall be corrected once and a second time for this. If he still do not amend, he shall not be allowed to share the common meal; but let him be separated from the company of the brethren and take his meal alone, and be deprived of his allowance of wine, until he do penance and amend. And let the same punishment be inflicted on him who is not present at the verse which is said after the meal. And let no one venture to take any food or drink before the appointed hour or afterwards. But if the superior offer a brother anything and he refuse it, then when he wants what he formerly refused or something else, let him receive nothing whatever, until he have made fitting amends.

CHAPTER

44

HOW THE EXCOMMUNICATED
ARE TO MAKE
SATISFACTION

L ET this be the rule for one who for a serious fault is excommunicated from oratory and table. At the hour when the Work of God is being performed in the oratory, let him lie prostrate before the door of the oratory, saying nothing, but just lying there with his face to the ground at the feet of the brethren as they come out of the oratory. And let him continue to do this until the abbot judge that he has made satisfaction for his offence. When at the abbot's bidding he has come into the oratory, let him throw himself first at the abbot's feet and then before the rest of the brethren, asking them to pray for him. And then, if the abbot so order, let him be received into the choir, to the place which the abbot shall appoint. Nevertheless, he must not presume to intone psalm, or lesson, or anything else in the oratory, unless the abbot give that further permission. And at every Hour, at the end of the Work of God, let him cast himself on the ground in the place where he stands; and let him make such satisfaction until the abbot order him anew that he should desist from it. But those who for slight faults are excommunicated from the table only, shall make satisfaction in the oratory at the abbot's good pleasure. Let them do penance until he blesses them and says "That will do."

CHAPTER

45

OF THOSE WHO
MAKE MISTAKES
IN THE ORATORY

I F anyone make a mistake in the recitation of psalm, responsory, antiphon, or lesson, and do not make humble satisfaction there before all, let him undergo greater punishment, because he would not repair by humility the fault that he committed through carelessness. But boys for such faults shall be whipped.

Mar. 25
July 25
Nov. 24

CHAPTER

46

OF THOSE WHO
OFFEND IN ANY
OTHER MATTERS

Mar. 26
July 26
Nov. 25

IF anyone in the course of his work, of whatever sort and in whatever place, be it while serving or in kitchen, store-room, bakehouse, garden, or anywhere else, shall commit any fault, or break anything, or lose anything, or fall into any transgression whatever, and do not come at once of his own accord to confess his offence to the abbot and community and do penance for it, but it become known through another: let him undergo greater punishment. However, should the matter be a secret sin of the soul, let him tell such a thing to the abbot alone, or to a spiritual father; for they know how to cure both their own wounds and the wounds of others without disclosing and publishing them.

CHAPTER

47

THE SIGNAL FOR
THE WORK
OF GOD

Mar. 27
July 27
Nov. 26

THE indicating of the hour for the Work of God by day and by night shall be the business of the abbot. Let him either do it himself or entrust the duty to such a careful brother that everything may be fulfilled at its proper time. The intoning of psalms and antiphons shall be done by those who are appointed for it, in their order after the abbot. But let no one presume to sing or read, unless he can fulfil the office to the edification of his hearers. Let it be done with humility, gravity, and reverence, and by him whom the abbot has appointed.

OF THE DAILY MANUAL LABOUR

IDLENESS is the enemy of the soul. The brethren, there- Mar. 28
fore, must be occupied at stated hours in manual July 28
labour, and again at other hours in sacred reading. To Nov. 27
this end we think that the times for each may be determined
in the following manner. From Easter until September the
14th, the brethren shall start work in the morning and from
the first hour until about the fourth do the tasks that have
to be done. From the fourth hour until about the sixth let
them apply themselves to reading. After the sixth hour,
having left the table, let them rest on their beds in perfect
silence; or if anyone wishes to read by himself, let him read
so as not to disturb the others. Let None be said early, at the
middle of the eighth hour; and let them again do what work
has to be done until Vespers. But if the circumstances of the
place or their poverty require them to gather the harvest
themselves, let them not be discontented; for then are they
truly monks when they live by the labour of their hands, like
our fathers and the apostles. Yet let all things be done in
moderation on account of the faint-hearted.

From September the 14th to the beginning of Lent, let Mar. 29
them apply themselves to reading up to the end of the second July 29
hour. Let Terce be said at that point, and from then until Nov. 28
None let them all work at the tasks appointed to them. As
soon as the first signal for None has been given, let them all
abandon their work and hold themselves ready for the
sounding of the second signal. After the meal let them apply
themselves to their reading or to the study of the psalms.

In the days of Lent let them apply themselves to their

53

reading from the morning until the end of the third hour,
and from then until the end of the tenth hour let them perform the work that is assigned to them. In these days of Lent
let them each receive a book from the library,[1] which they
shall read through consecutively; let these books be given
out at the beginning of Lent. But one or two senior monks
should certainly be deputed to go round the monastery at
the times when the brethren are occupied in reading, to see
that there be no slothful brother who spends his time in
idleness or gossip and neglects the reading, so that he not
only does himself harm but also disturbs others. If there be
such a one (which God forbid), let him be corrected once
and a second time; if he do not amend, let him undergo the
punishment of the Rule, so that the rest may be afraid. And
the brethren should not associate with one another at un-
seasonable hours.

Mar. 30
July 30
Nov. 29

On Sundays likewise all shall apply themselves to reading,
except those who are assigned to various duties. But if there
be anyone so careless and slothful that he will not or cannot
study or read, let him be given some work to perform, so
that he may not be idle. Sick or delicate brethren should be
assigned a task or craft of such a kind that on the one hand
they be not idle, and on the other be not overborne by ex-
cessive toil or[2] driven away from the monastery. The abbot
should have consideration for their weakness.

[1] Note 108.   [2] The *aut* of the Latin text may be equivalent to *et*, so that we
could put "and" here. Note 38.

CHAPTER

49

OF THE OBSERVANCE
OF LENT

THE life of a monk ought at all times to be lenten in its character; but since few have the strength for that, we therefore urge that in these days of Lent the brethren should lead lives of great purity, and should also in this sacred season expiate the negligences of other times. This will be worthily done if we refrain from all sin and apply ourselves to prayer with tears, to reading, to compunction of heart, and to abstinence. In these days, therefore, let us add something beyond the wonted measure of our service, such as private prayers and abstinence in food and drink. Let each one, over and above the measure prescribed for him, offer God something of his own free will in the joy of the Holy Spirit. That is to say, let him stint himself of food, drink, sleep, talk, and jesting, and look forward with the joy of spiritual longing to the holy feast of Easter. Let each one, however, tell his abbot what he is offering, and let it be done with his consent and blessing; because what is done without the permission of the spiritual father shall be ascribed to presumption and vainglory and not reckoned meritorious. Everything, therefore, is to be done with the approval of the abbot.

Mar. 31
July 31
Nov. 30

CHAPTER

50

OF BRETHREN WHO ARE
WORKING FAR FROM THE
ORATORY OR JOURNEYING

Apr. 1
Aug. 1
Dec. 1

I F any brethren be at work at a great distance, so that they cannot get to the oratory at the proper time, and if the abbot recognize that such is the case, then let them perform the Work of God in the place where they are working, bending their knees in reverence before God. In like manner let those who are sent on a journey not miss the appointed Hours; but let them say them for themselves, as well as they can, and not neglect to pay the due measure of their service.

CHAPTER

51

OF BRETHREN WHO
DO NOT GO
VERY FAR

Apr. 2
Aug. 2
Dec. 2

I F a brother be sent out on some business and be expected to return to the monastery that same day, let him not presume to eat while abroad, even though he be urgently pressed to do so, unless his abbot have so bidden him. If he do otherwise, let him be excommunicated.

CHAPTER

52

OF THE ORATORY
OF THE MONASTERY

Apr. 3
Aug. 3
Dec. 3

LET the oratory be what its name implies, and let nothing else be done or kept there. When the Work of God is finished, let all go out in deep silence, and let reverence for God be observed, so that any brother who may wish to pray privately be not hindered by another's mis-behaviour. And at other times also, if anyone wish to pray secretly, let him just go in and pray: not in a loud voice, but with tears and fervour of heart. He, therefore, who does not behave so, shall not be permitted to remain in the oratory when the Work of God is ended, lest he should, as we have said, be a hindrance to another.

CHAPTER

53

OF THE RECEPTION
OF GUESTS

Apr. 4
Aug. 4
Dec. 4

LET all guests that come be received like Christ, for he will say: *I was a stranger and ye took me in.*[1] And let fitting honour be shown to all, but especially to churchmen and pilgrims. As soon, therefore, as a guest is announced, let the superior or some brethren meet him with all charitable service. And first of all let them pray together, and then let them unite in the kiss of peace. This kiss of peace shall not be offered until after the prayers have been said, on account of the delusions of the devil. In the greeting of all guests, whether they be arriving or departing, let the greatest humility be shown. Let the head be bowed

[1] Mat. xxv. 35.

or the whole body prostrated on the ground, and so let Christ be worshipped in them, for indeed he is received in their persons.

When the guests have been received, let them be led to prayer, and afterwards let the superior, or a monk appointed by him, sit with them. Let the law of God be read before the guest for his edification, and then let all kindness be shown to him. The superior shall break his fast for the sake of a guest, unless it be a special fast day which may not be violated; but the brethren shall observe the customary fasts. Let the abbot give the guests water for their hands; and let both abbot and community wash the feet of all guests. When they have washed them, let them say this verse: *Suscepimus, Deus, misericordiam tuam in medio templi tui.*[1] In the reception of poor men and pilgrims special attention should be shown, because in them is Christ more truly welcomed; for the fear which the rich inspire is enough of itself to secure them honour.

Apr. 5
Aug. 5
Dec. 5

Let there be a separate kitchen for the abbot and guests, so that the brethren may not be disturbed when guests— who are never lacking in a monastery—arrive at irregular hours. There shall be appointed to this kitchen by the year two brethren who can discharge the duty well. Let help be given them according as they need it, so that they may serve without murmuring. And, on the other hand, when they have less to do, let them go out to whatever task is assigned to them. And not only to them, but to all the officials of the monastery, let the same consideration be shown and help given whenever it is needed; and, on the other hand, when they are unoccupied, let them do whatever they are bidden.

The guest-house shall be assigned to a brother whose soul

[1] Ps. xlvii. 10.

is full of the fear of God. Let there be a sufficient number of beds ready therein. And let the house of God be administered by prudent men in a prudent manner.

Let no one, without special instructions, associate or converse with guests. If he meet or see them, let him greet them humbly, as we have said, and ask a blessing; then let him pass on, saying that he is not permitted to talk with a guest.

CHAPTER
54

WHETHER A MONK SHOULD RECEIVE LETTERS OR ANYTHING ELSE

O^N no account shall a monk be allowed to receive letters, devout tokens, or any small gifts whatsoever, from his parents or other people or his brethren, or to give the same, without the abbot's permission. But if he have been sent anything even by his parents, let him not presume to take it before it has been shown to the abbot. If the abbot allow it to be received, it shall be his to decide to whom it is to be given; and let not the brother, to whom it was sent, be vexed thereat, lest occasion be given to the devil. Should anyone presume to act otherwise, let him undergo the punishment of the Rule.

Apr. 6
Aug. 6
Dec. 6

CHAPTER

55

THE CLOTHES
AND SHOES OF
THE BRETHREN

Apr. 7
Aug. 7
Dec. 7

LET clothing be given to the brethren according to the nature of the locality in which they dwell and its climate; for in cold districts they will need more clothing, and in warm districts less. It is the abbot's business to take thought for this matter. But we believe that in ordinary places the following dress is sufficient for each monk: a tunic, a cowl (thick and woolly in winter, but thin or worn in summer), a belt for work, and for the feet shoes and stockings. And let not the monks complain of the colour or coarseness of any of these things, but be content with what is to be found in the district where they live and can be purchased cheaply.

Let the abbot see to the size of the garments, that they be not too short for their wearers, but of the proper fit. When the brethren receive new clothes, let them always return the old ones at once, that they may be stored in the clothes-room for the poor. For it is sufficient if a monk have two tunics and two cowls, to allow for a change at night and for the washing of these garments; more than that is superfluity and should be curtailed. And let them return their stockings, and anything else that is old, when they receive new ones. Those who are sent on a journey shall receive drawers from the clothes-room, which they shall wash and restore when they return. And let their cowls and tunics be somewhat better than the ones they wear usually. They shall receive them from the clothes-room when they are starting on their journey and restore them when they return.

For bedding, let this suffice: a mattress, a blanket, a coverlet, and a pillow. The beds should be examined frequently by the abbot, lest any private property be concealed in them. If any brother be found to have anything that he has not received from the abbot, let him undergo the strictest punishment. And in order that this evil of private ownership may be rooted out utterly, let the abbot provide all things that are necessary: that is, cowl, tunic, stockings, shoes, belt, knife, pen, needle, handkerchief, and tablets; so that all pretext of need may be taken away. Yet let the abbot always consider those words of the Acts of the Apostles: *Distribution was made to everyone according as he had need.*[1] So too let the abbot consider the weaknesses of the needy, and not the ill-will of the jealous. But in all his decisions let him think upon the retribution of God.

Apr. 8
Aug. 8
Dec. 8

CHAPTER

56

OF THE ABBOT'S TABLE

LET the abbot always eat with the guests and pilgrims. But when there are no guests, let him have the power to invite whom he will of the brethren. Yet, for discipline's sake, let one or two seniors always be left with the brethren.

Apr. 9
Aug. 9
Dec. 9

[1] Acts iv. 35.

CHAPTER

57

THE CRAFTSMEN OF THE MONASTERY

Apr. 10
Aug. 10
Dec. 10

IF there be craftsmen in the monastery, let them practise their crafts with all humility, provided the abbot give permission. But if one of them be puffed up because of his skill in his craft, supposing that he is conferring a benefit on the monastery, let him be removed from his work and not return to it, unless he have humbled himself and the abbot entrust it to him again. If any of the work of the craftsmen is to be sold, let those who have to manage the business take care that they be not guilty of any dishonesty. Let them always remember Ananias and Saphira, and take care lest they, or any others who deal dishonestly with the property of the monastery, should suffer in their souls the death which they endured in their bodies. And, as regards the price, let not the sin of avarice creep in; but let the goods always be sold a little cheaper than they are sold by people of the world, *that in all things God may be glorified.*[1]

CHAPTER

58

THE ORDER FOR THE RECEPTION OF BRETHREN

Apr. 11
Aug. 11
Dec. 11

WHEN anyone newly cometh to be a monk, let him not be granted an easy admittance; but, as the apostle saith: *Test the spirits, to see whether they come from God.*[2] If such a one, therefore, persevere in his knocking, and if it be seen after four or five days that he bears patiently his harsh treatment and the difficulty of admission

[1] 1 Peter iv. 11.   [2] 1 John iv. 1.

and persists in his petition, then let admittance be granted to him, and let him stay in the guest-house for a few days. After that let him dwell in the noviciate, where the novices work, eat, and sleep. And let a senior be assigned to them who is skilled in winning souls, that he may watch over them with the utmost care. Let him examine whether the novice truly seeks God, and whether he is zealous for the Work of God, for obedience, and for humiliations. Let him be told all the hardships and trials through which we travel to God.

If he promise to persevere in his purpose, then at the end of two months let this Rule be read through to him, and let him be addressed thus: "Behold the law under which you wish to serve; if you can observe it, enter; if you cannot, freely depart." If he still abide, then let him be led back into the aforesaid noviciate and again tested in all patience. After the lapse of six months let the Rule be read to him, so that he may know on what he is entering. And, if he still abide, after four months let the Rule be read to him again. And if, upon mature deliberation, he promise to observe all things and to obey all the commands that are given him, then let him be received into the community. But let him understand that according to the law of the Rule he is no longer free to leave the monastery, or to withdraw his neck from under the yoke of the Rule, which it was open to him, during that prolonged deliberation, either to refuse or to accept.

Now this shall be the manner of his reception. In the oratory, in the presence of all, he shall promise stability, conversion of his life, and obedience; and this before God and his Saints, so that he may know that should he ever do otherwise he will be condemned by him whom he mocks.

Apr. 12
Aug. 12
Dec. 12

He shall embody this promise of his in a petition, drawn up in the names of the Saints whose relics are there and of the abbot who is present. Let him write this document with his own hand; or, if he cannot write, let another do it at his request, and let the novice put his mark to it and place it on the altar with his own hand. When he has placed it there, let the novice himself at once intone this verse: *Suscipe me, Domine, secundum eloquium tuum, et vivam: et ne confundas me ab exspectatione mea.*[1] Let the whole community repeat this after him three times, adding at the end of all the *Gloria Patri*. Then let the novice prostrate himself before the feet of each monk, asking them to pray for him; and from that day let him be counted as one of the community. If he possess any property, let him either give it beforehand to the poor, or make a formal donation bestowing it on the monastery. Let him keep back nothing at all for himself, as knowing that thenceforward he will not have the disposition even of his own body. So let him, there and then in the oratory, be stripped of his own clothes which he is wearing and dressed in the clothes of the monastery. But let those clothes, which have been taken off him, be put aside in the clothes-room and kept there. Then, should he ever listen to the persuasions of the devil and decide to leave the monastery (which God forbid), let them take off him the clothes of the monastery and so dismiss him. But his petition, which the abbot took from off the altar, shall not be returned to him, but shall be preserved in the monastery.

[1] Ps. cxviii. 116.

59

THE OFFERING OF THE SONS
OF THE RICH AND
OF THE POOR

I F any man of good station offer his son to God in the
monastery and the boy himself be still very young, let
his parents draw up the petition which we mentioned
above. And then at the Offertory let them wrap the petition
and the boy's hand in the altar cloth and so offer him. As
regards his property, let them promise in the same document under oath that they will never of themselves, or
through an intermediary, or in any way whatever, give him
anything or provide him with the opportunity of possessing
anything. But if they prefer not to do this and desire to give
an alms to the monastery for their advantage, let them draw
up a deed of gift of the property which they desire to give
to the monastery, reserving the income to themselves if they
wish. And in this way let every opening be stopped, so that
the boy may have no expectations whereby (which God forbid) he might be deceived and ruined, as we have learnt by
experience. And let poorer folk do in like manner. But those
who possess nothing at all, shall simply draw up the petition
and offer their son at the Offertory in the presence of wit-
nesses.

Apr. 13
Aug. 13
Dec. 13

CHAPTER

60

OF PRIESTS WHO MAY
WISH TO DWELL IN
THE MONASTERY

Apr. 14
Aug. 14
Dec. 14

IF anyone of the priestly order ask to be received into the monastery, permission shall not be granted him too readily. Nevertheless, if he persevere firmly in his petition, let him know that he will have to observe the full discipline of the Rule and that nothing will be abated for him. As the Scripture saith : *Friend, whereunto art thou come?*[1] However, let him be allowed to take rank next to the abbot, to pronounce blessings, and to celebrate Mass, provided that the abbot give him permission. Otherwise, let him not presume to do anything, knowing that he is subject to the discipline of the Rule ; but rather let him give to all an example of humility. If there be question of an appointment or of some business in the monastery, let him hold the place that is his according to the date of his entrance into the monastery, and not that which is granted to him out of respect for his priesthood. If any clerics, likewise, should desire to become members of the community, let them be assigned a middle rank. Yet they too are to be admitted only on condition that they promise observance of the Rule and their stability.

[1] Mat. xxvi. 50.

HOW PILGRIM
MONKS ARE TO
BE RECEIVED

I F a pilgrim monk come from a distant region and desire to dwell in the monastery as a guest, let him be received for as long a time as he wishes, provided that he is content with the customs of the place as they are, and does not disturb the monastery by exorbitant wants, but is simply content with what he finds. Should he reasonably, modestly, and charitably censure or remark upon any defect, let the abbot consider the matter prudently, lest perchance the Lord have sent him for this very end. And if later on he should wish to bind himself to stability, let not his desire be denied him, especially as the character of his life could be discerned during the time that he was a guest.

Apr. 15
Aug. 15
Dec. 15

But if during that time he be found exacting or depraved, not only should he not be made a member of the community, but he should be told politely to depart, lest others should be corrupted by his lamentable life. If, however, he do not deserve to be dismissed, not only should he be received on his asking as a member of the community, but he should even be urged to stay, so that others may be instructed by his example, and because wherever we are we serve the same Lord and fight for the same King. And the abbot may even give him a higher place in the community, if he consider him worthy of it. And so also, not only with a monk, but also with the aforesaid orders of priests and clerics: the abbot may give them a rank higher than is theirs by their entry, if he see that their life deserves it. But let the abbot beware lest he ever receive a monk of some other known monastery as a member of his community without the consent of his

Apr. 16
Aug. 16
Dec. 16

67

abbot and a letter of recommendation, because it is written:
*Do not thou to another what thou wouldst not have done to
thyself.* [1]

Apr. 17
Aug. 17
Dec. 17

IF any abbot wish to have a priest or a deacon ordained for
his monastery, let him choose out one of his subjects
who is worthy to exercise the priestly office. But let the
one who is ordained beware of elation or pride; and let him
not presume to do anything but what is commanded him by
the abbot, knowing that he will be all the more subject to
the discipline of the monastery. Let him not because of his
priesthood forget the obedience and discipline of the Rule,
but make ever more and more progress towards God.

Let him always keep the place which is his according to
the time of his entry into the monastery, except in his duties
at the altar, and unless he have been promoted by the vote of
the community and the abbot's decision, on account of the
worthiness of his life. Yet let him understand that he must
observe the injunctions laid down for deans and priors.
Should he presume to act otherwise, let him be judged not
a priest but a rebel; and if after frequent admonitions he do
not amend, let the bishop's authority be invoked. If he do
not amend even then but is manifestly culpable, let him be
dismissed from the monastery; provided that his contumacy
be such that he refuses to submit and to obey the Rule.

[1] Tob. iv. 16.

63

THE ORDER OF
THE COMMUNITY

Apr. 18
Aug. 18
Dec. 18

THE brethren shall keep their order in the monastery according to the date of their entry, or according to the merit of their lives and as the abbot shall determine. Yet the abbot must not disturb the flock committed to him, nor by an exercise of arbitrary authority ordain anything unjustly; but let him always consider that he will have to render God an account of all his judgements and deeds. Let the brethren, therefore, receive the kiss of peace, go to Communion, intone the psalms, and stand in choir according to the order which the abbot has determined or which they have of themselves. And on no occasion whatever should age distinguish the brethren and decide their order; for Samuel and Daniel, though young, judged the elders. Therefore, excepting those already mentioned, whom the abbot has by special decision promoted or for definite reasons degraded, all shall take their order according to the time of their entry. Let him, for instance, who came to the monastery at the second hour of the day (whatever be his age or dignity), know that he is junior to him who came at the first hour. Boys, however, are to be kept under discipline at all times and by every one.

Apr. 19
Aug. 19
Dec. 19

The juniors, therefore, shall honour their seniors, and the seniors love their juniors. In addressing one another let them never use the bare name; but let a senior call his junior "Brother", and a junior call his senior "Nonnus", which signifies "Reverend Father". But let the abbot, since he is believed to hold the place of Christ, be called Lord and Abbot, not for any pretensions of his own, but for the honour and love of Christ. Let the abbot himself be mindful of this, and behave so that he may be worthy of such honour. Wherever the brethren meet one another, let the junior ask the senior for his blessing. When a senior passes by, let a junior rise and make room for him to seat himself; nor let the junior presume to sit down, unless his senior bid him, so that the Scripture may be fulfilled: *Be eager to give one another precedence.* [1] Boys and youths shall keep strictly to their order in the oratory and at table. Everywhere else let them have supervision and discipline, until they come to the age of discretion.

CHAPTER

64

THE APPOINTMENT
OF THE ABBOT

Apr. 20
Aug. 20
Dec. 20

I N the appointment of the abbot let this rule always be observed, that he be made abbot who is chosen unanimously in the fear of God by the whole community, or even by a minority, however small, if its counsel be more wholesome. Let him who is to be appointed be chosen for the merit of his life and his enlightened wisdom, even though he be the last in order of the community. But if (which God forbid) the whole community should agree to choose a person who acquiesces in its vices, and if these somehow come to the knowledge of the local bishop and neighbouring abbots or christians, let them foil this conspiracy of the wicked and set a worthy steward over God's house. Let

[1] Rom. xii. 10.

70

them be sure that they will receive a good reward, if they do this with a pure intention and out of zeal for God, just as, on the contrary, they will incur sin, if they neglect to intervene.

Let the abbot when appointed consider always what an office he has undertaken and to whom he must render an account of his stewardship; and let him know that it is his duty rather to profit his brethren than to preside over them. It behoves him, therefore, to be learned in the divine law, so that he may have a treasure of knowledge whence he may bring forth things new and old; and to be chaste, sober, and merciful. Let him always *set mercy above judgement*[1] so that he himself may obtain mercy. Let him hate ill-doing but love the brethren. In administering correction, let him act with prudent moderation, lest being too zealous in removing the rust he break the vessel. Let him always distrust his own frailty and remember that the bruised reed is not to be broken. By this we do not mean that he should allow evils to grow, but that, as we have said above, he should eradicate them prudently and with charity, in the way which may seem best in each case. And let him study rather to be loved than feared. Let him not be turbulent or anxious, overbearing or obstinate, jealous or too suspicious, for otherwise he will never be at rest. Let him be prudent and considerate in all his commands; and whether the work which he enjoins concern God or the world, let him always be discreet and moderate, bearing in mind the discretion of holy Jacob, who said: *If I cause my flocks to be overdriven, they will all perish in one day.*[2] So, imitating these and other examples of discretion, the mother of the virtues, let him so temper all things that the strong may still have something to long after, and

Apr. 21
Aug. 21
Dec. 21

---

[1] *Cf.* James ii. 13.   [2] Gen. xxxiii. 13.

the weak may not draw back in alarm. And, especially, let him keep this present Rule in all things; so that having ministered faithfully he may hear from the Lord what the good servant heard who gave his fellow-servants wheat in due season: *Amen, I say unto you, he will set him over all his goods.* [1]

CHAPTER

65

THE PRIOR OF THE MONASTERY

Apr. 22
Aug. 22
Dec. 22
IT frequently happens that the appointment of a prior gives rise to serious scandals in monasteries. For there are men puffed up by an evil spirit of pride who regard themselves as equal to the abbot, and arrogating to themselves tyrannical power foster troubles and dissensions in the community. This happens especially in those places where the prior is appointed by the same bishop and the same abbots as the abbot himself. But it is very clear that this is a foolish procedure. For it gives the prior matter for pride from the very beginning of his appointment, since his thoughts will suggest to him that he is not subject to the abbot: "For," he will say to himself, "you were appointed by the same people that appointed the abbot." Hence arise envies, quarrels, detractions, rivalries, dissensions, and disorders. For, while the abbot and prior are at variance, it must needs be that their souls are endangered by this dissension. And their subjects also, currying favour with this side or that, run headlong to perdition. The responsibility for this dangerous state of affairs rests ultimately on those whose action caused such disorder.

[1] Mat. xxiv. 47.

Therefore, we have judged it expedient, for the preser- Apr. 23
vation of peace and of charity, that the abbot should have the Aug. 23
appointment to all offices in his monastery. If it be possible, Dec. 23
let all the affairs of the monastery be administered by deans
under the control of the abbot, as we have already arranged.
The business being thus shared by many, no individual will
become proud. But if the circumstances of the place require
it, or the community reasonably and humbly ask for it, and
the abbot judge that it is expedient, let him himself appoint
as his prior whomsoever he may choose, with the advice of
God-fearing brethren. Let the prior respectfully perform
what is enjoined him by his abbot, and do nothing contrary
to the abbot's will or regulations; for the more he is set
above the rest, the more scrupulously should he observe the
precepts of the Rule. If it should be found that the prior has
serious faults, or that he is deceived by pride and behaves
arrogantly, or if he should be proved to be a despiser of the
holy Rule, he shall be verbally admonished up to four times;
if he do not amend, let the punishment of the Rule be applied
to him. But if he do not amend even then, let him be deposed
from the office of prior and another who is worthy be appointed in his place. But if afterwards he be not quiet and
obedient in the community, let him even be expelled from
the monastery. Yet let the abbot bear in mind that he must
give God an account of all his judgements, lest perchance
his mind be inflamed by the fire of envy or jealousy.

66

THE PORTERS OF
THE MONASTERY

Apr. 24
Aug. 24
Dec. 24

A T the gate of the monastery let there be placed a wise old man, who understands how to give and receive a message, and whose years will keep him from leaving his post. This porter should have a room near the gate, so that those who come may always find someone to answer them. As soon as anyone knocks, or a poor man hails him, let him answer *Deo gratias* or *Benedic*. Then let him attend to them promptly, with all the gentleness of the fear of God and with fervent charity. If the porter need help, let him have one of the younger brethren.

The monastery should, if possible, be so arranged that all necessary things, such as water, mill, garden, and various crafts may be within the enclosure, so that the monks may not be compelled to wander outside it, for that is not at all expedient for their souls.

We desire that this Rule be read aloud often in the community, so that no brother may excuse himself on the ground of ignorance.

67

OF BRETHREN
WHO ARE SENT
ON A JOURNEY

Apr. 25
Aug. 25
Dec. 25

L ET brethren who are to be sent on a journey commend themselves to the prayers of all the brethren and of the abbot; and always at the last prayer of the Work of God let there be a commemoration of all absent brethren. When brethren return from a journey, let them on the day they return, at the end of each canonical Hour of the Work of God, lie prostrate on the floor of the oratory and ask the prayers of all on account of any faults that may have surprised them on the road, by the seeing or hearing of something evil, or by idle talk. Nor let anyone presume to tell another what he has seen or heard outside the monastery, because this causes very great harm. But if anyone presume to do so, let him undergo the punishment of the Rule. And let him be punished likewise who shall presume to leave the enclosure of the monastery, or to go anywhere, or to do anything however trifling, without the permission of the abbot.

CHAPTER

68

IF A BROTHER BE COMMANDED TO DO IMPOSSIBLE THINGS

I F it happen that something hard or impossible be laid upon any brother, let him receive the command of his superior with all docility and obedience. But if he see that the weight of the burden altogether exceeds the measure of his strength, let him explain the reasons of his incapacity to his superior calmly and in due season, without pride, obstinacy, or contentiousness. If after his representations the superior still persist in his decision and command, let the subject know that it is expedient for him, and let him obey out of love, trusting in the assistance of God.

Apr. 26
Aug. 26
Dec. 26

THAT THE MONKS PRESUME NOT TO DEFEND ONE ANOTHER

Apr. 27
Aug. 27
Dec. 27

CARE must be taken that no monk venture on any ground to defend another monk in the monastery, or as it were to take him under his protection, even though they be connected by some tie of kinship. Let not the monks venture to do this in any way whatsoever, because it may give rise to most serious scandals. But if anyone break this rule, let him be punished very severely.

THAT NO ONE VENTURE TO PUNISH AT RANDOM

Apr. 28
Aug. 28
Dec. 28

EVERY occasion of presumption should be avoided in the monastery. So we decree that no one be allowed to excommunicate or strike any of his brethren, except the abbot have given him authority. *Let those that offend be reproved before all, that the rest may have fear.*[1] However, boys up to fifteen years of age shall be carefully controlled and watched by all, yet this too with all moderation and prudence. But if anyone venture without the abbot's instructions to punish those of riper years, or to treat the boys with immoderate severity, let him undergo the discipline of the Rule, for it is written: *Do not thou to another, what thou wouldst not have done to thyself.*[2]

[1] 1 Tim. v. 20. [2] Tob. iv. 16.

CHAPTER
71

THAT THE BRETHREN
BE OBEDIENT TO
ONE ANOTHER

Apr. 29
Aug. 29
Dec. 29

Not only shall the virtue of obedience be practised by all towards the abbot, but the brethren shall also obey one another, knowing that by this road of obedience will they go to God. The commands of the abbot or of the superiors appointed by him must rank first, and no unofficial commands take precedence of them; but, for the rest, let all the juniors obey their seniors with all love and diligence. If anyone be found quarrelsome, let him be corrected. And if any brother, for however trifling a reason, be corrected in any way by the abbot, or any of his seniors, or if he perceive that any senior, in however small a degree, is displeased or angry with him, let him at once without delay cast himself on the ground at his feet, and lie there making reparation, until that displeasure is appeased and he bless him. But if anyone should disdain to do this, let him either undergo corporal punishment, or, if he be stubborn, let him be expelled from the monastery.

CHAPTER
72

OF THE GOOD ZEAL
WHICH MONKS
OUGHT TO HAVE

Apr. 30
Aug. 30
Dec. 30

Just as there is an evil zeal of bitterness which separates from God and leads to hell, so is there a good zeal which separates from evil and leads to God and life everlasting. Let monks, therefore, exercise this zeal with the most fervent love. Let them, that is, *give one another prece-*

dence.[1] Let them bear with the greatest patience one another's infirmities, whether of body or character. Let them vie in paying obedience one to another. Let none follow what seems good for himself, but rather what is good for another. Let them practise fraternal charity with a pure love. Let them fear God. Let them love their abbot with a sincere and humble affection. Let them prefer nothing whatever to Christ. And may he bring us all alike to life everlasting.

CHAPTER

73

THAT THE FULL OBSERVANCE OF JUSTICE IS NOT ESTABLISHED IN THIS RULE

May   1
Aug. 31
Dec. 31

THIS Rule has been written in order that, by practising it in monasteries, we may show that we have attained some degree of virtue and the rudiments of monastic observance. But, for him who would hasten to the perfection of the monastic life, there are the teachings of the holy Fathers, by observing which a man is led to the summit of perfection. For what page or what utterance of the divinely-inspired books of the Old and the New Testament is not a most unerring rule of human life? Or what book of the holy Catholic Fathers is not manifestly devoted to teaching us the straight road to our Creator? Then the Conferences of Cassian and his Institutes, and the Lives of the Fathers, as also the Rule of our holy father Basil: what else are they but tools of virtue for good-living and obedient monks? But we slothful, ill-living, and negligent people must blush for shame. Whoever, therefore, thou art that hastenest to thy

[1] Rom. xii. 10.

heavenly country, fulfil first of all by the help of Christ this little Rule for beginners. And then at length, under God's protection, shalt thou attain those aforesaid loftier heights of wisdom and virtue.

THE END